Real World

Colouring Book

For Advanced Users & Adults

50 Images

**Created From Real Life Photos
For You To Colour As You Please.**

ISBN 978-0-359-79379-2
90000
9 780359 793792

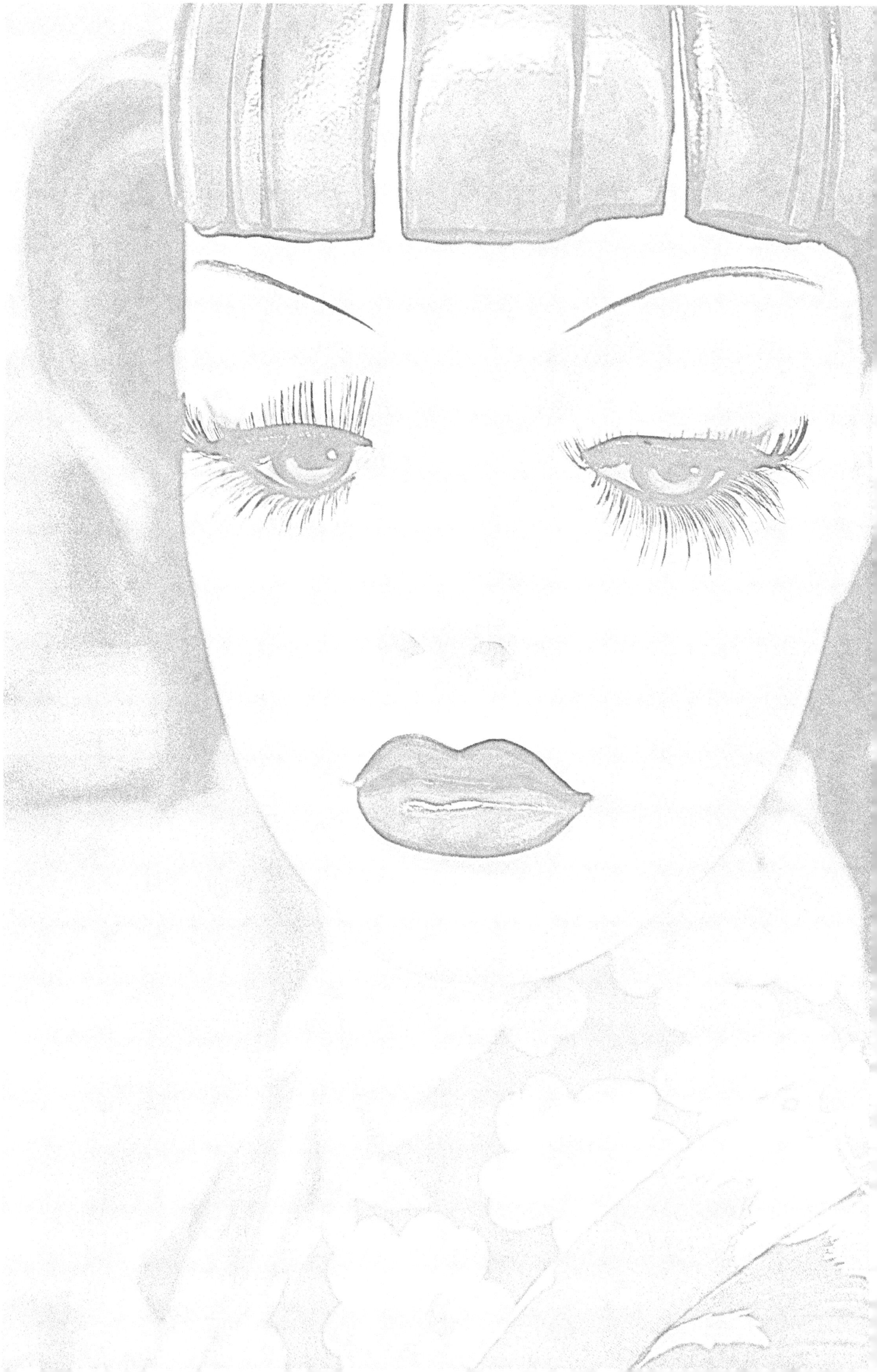

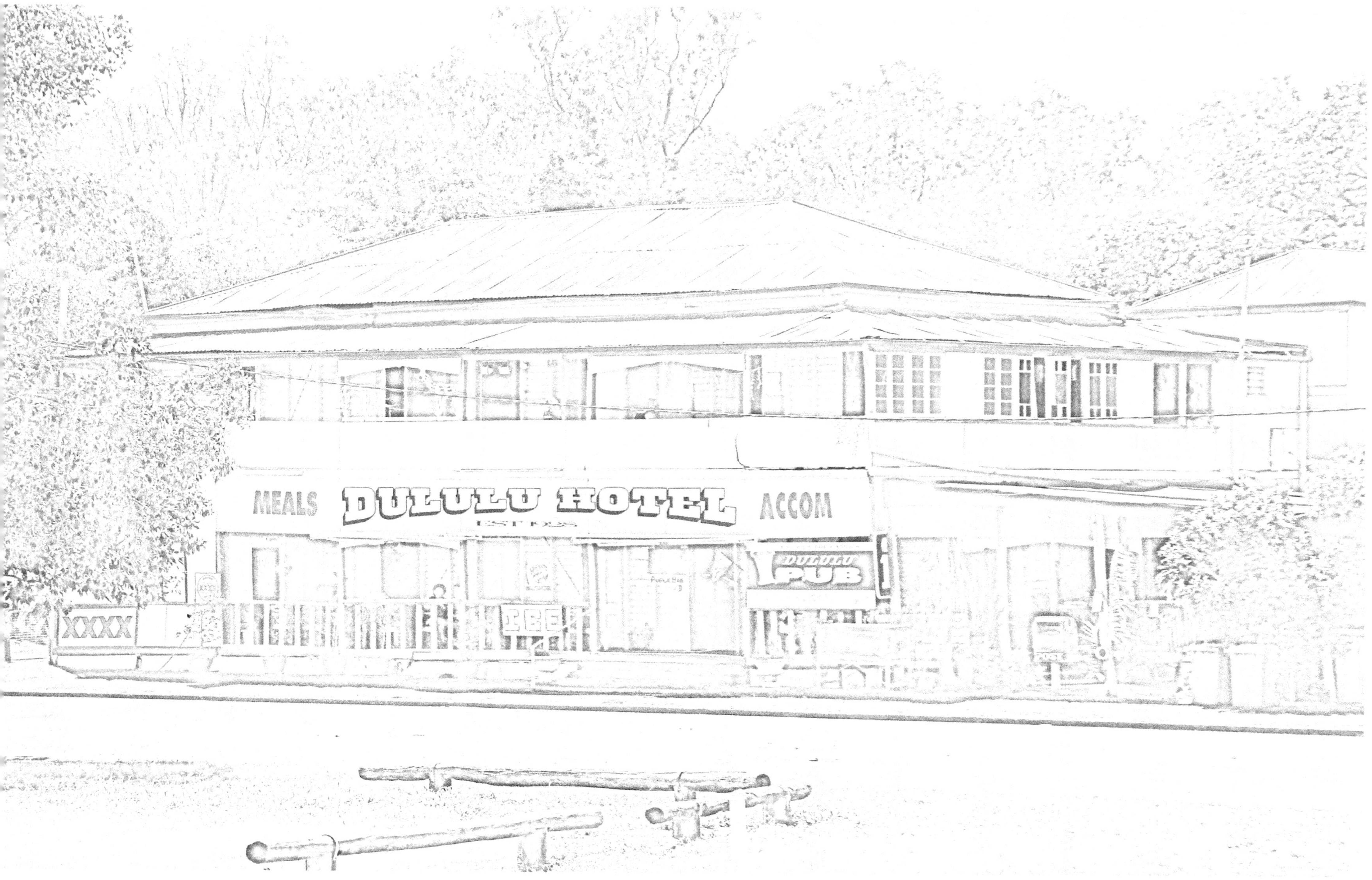
MEALS
DULULU HOTEL
ACCOM
DULULU PUB
XXXX

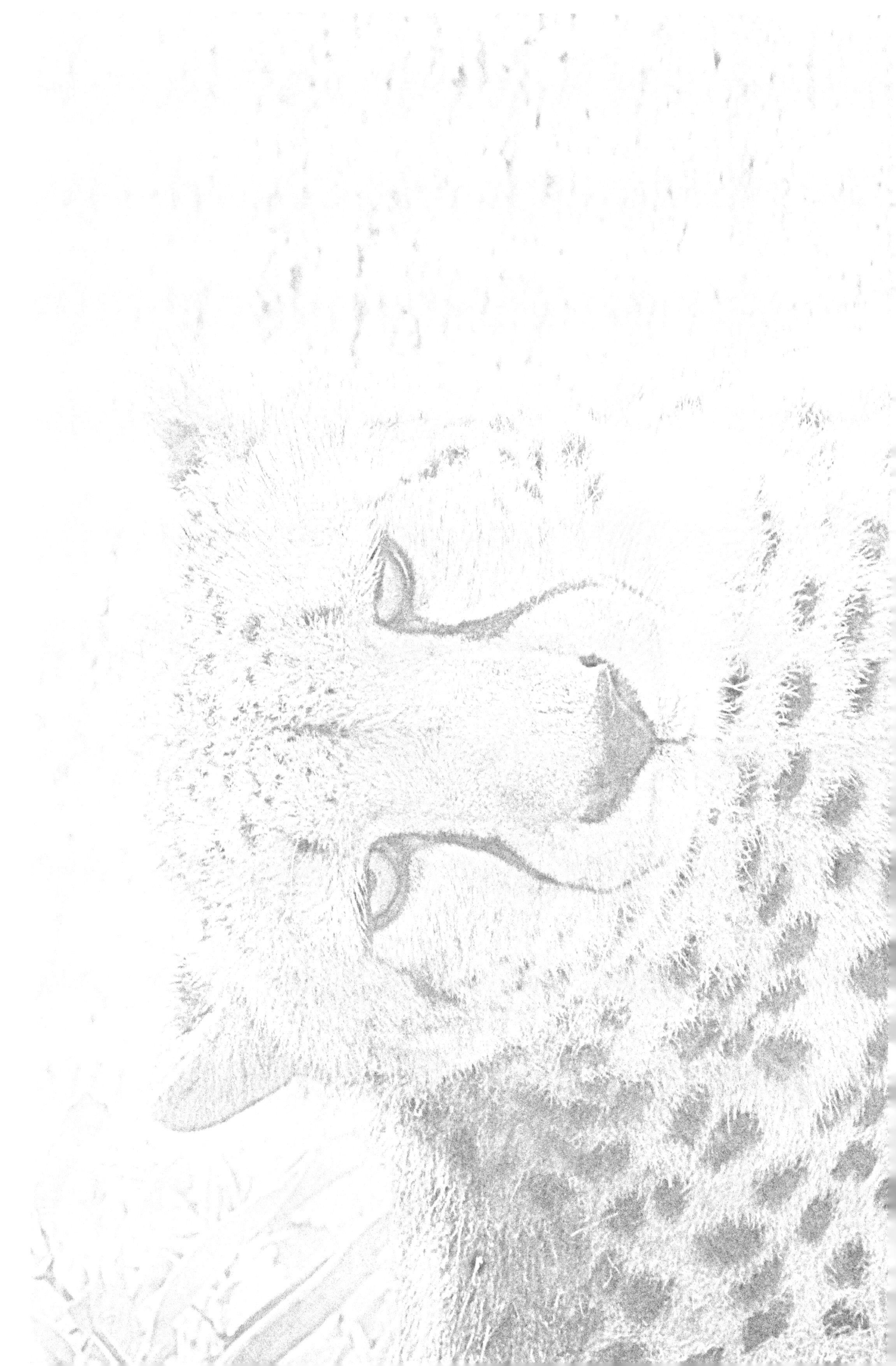

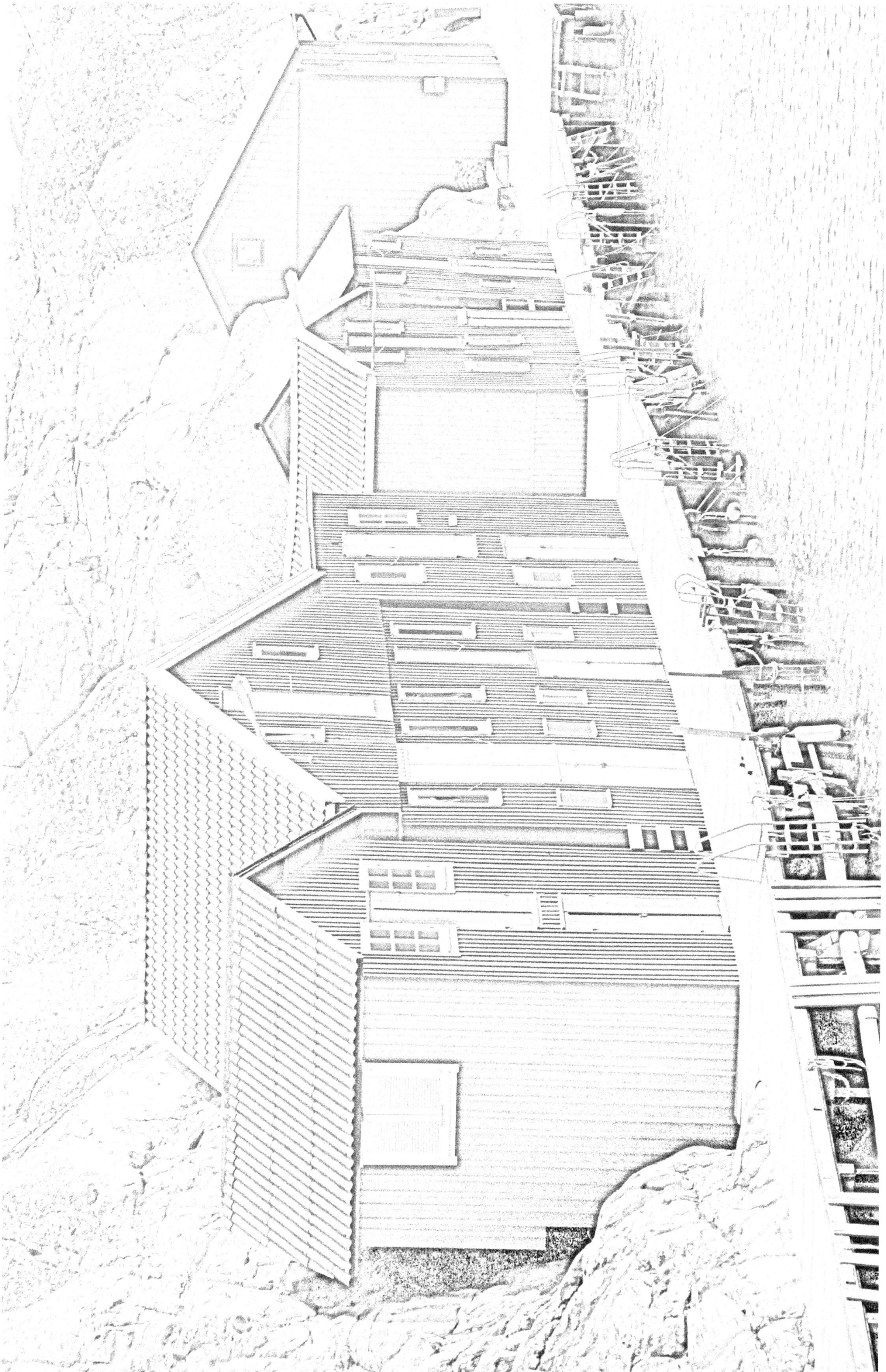

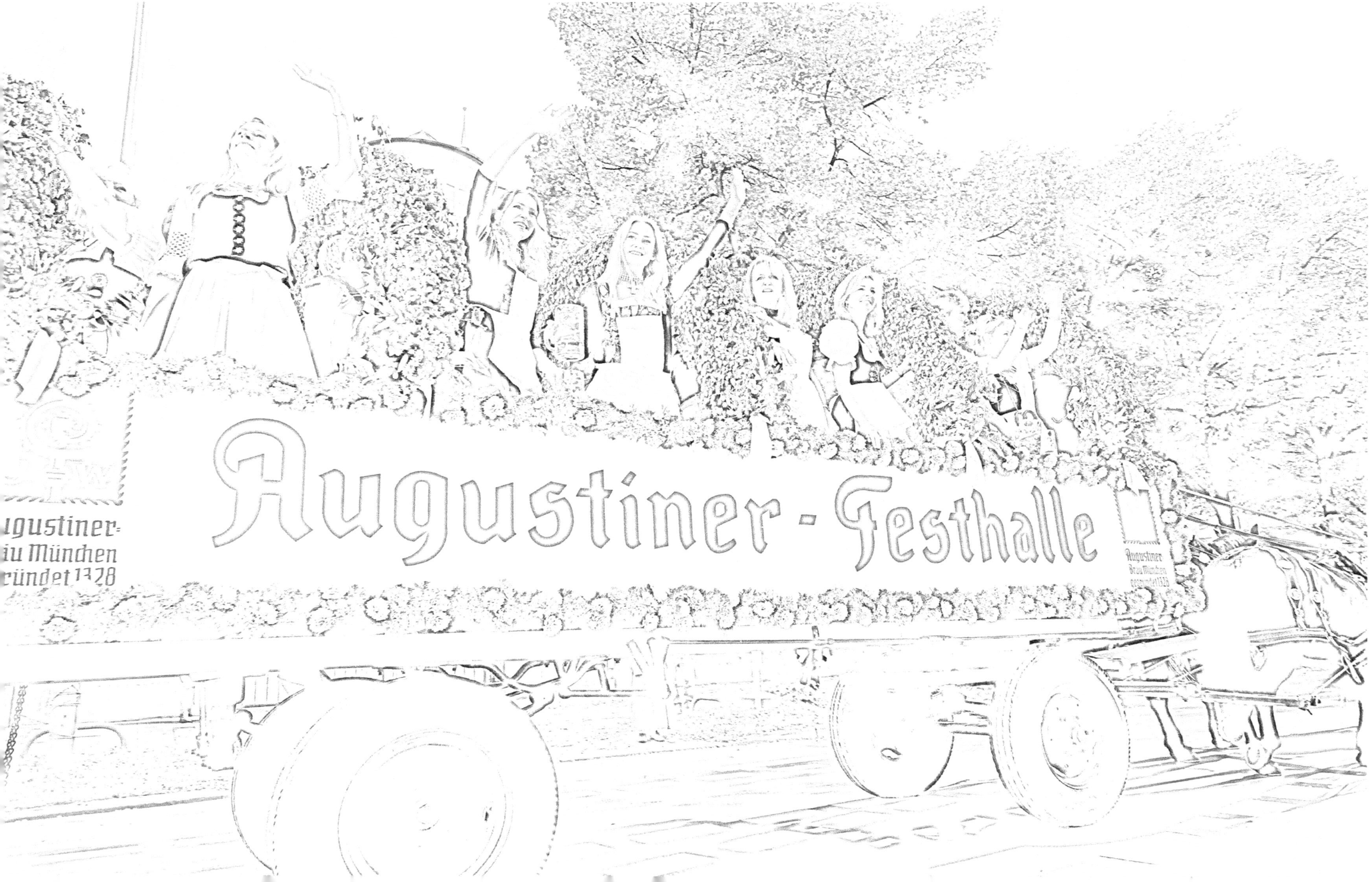
Augustiner - Festhalle
ugustiner-
u München
ründet 1328

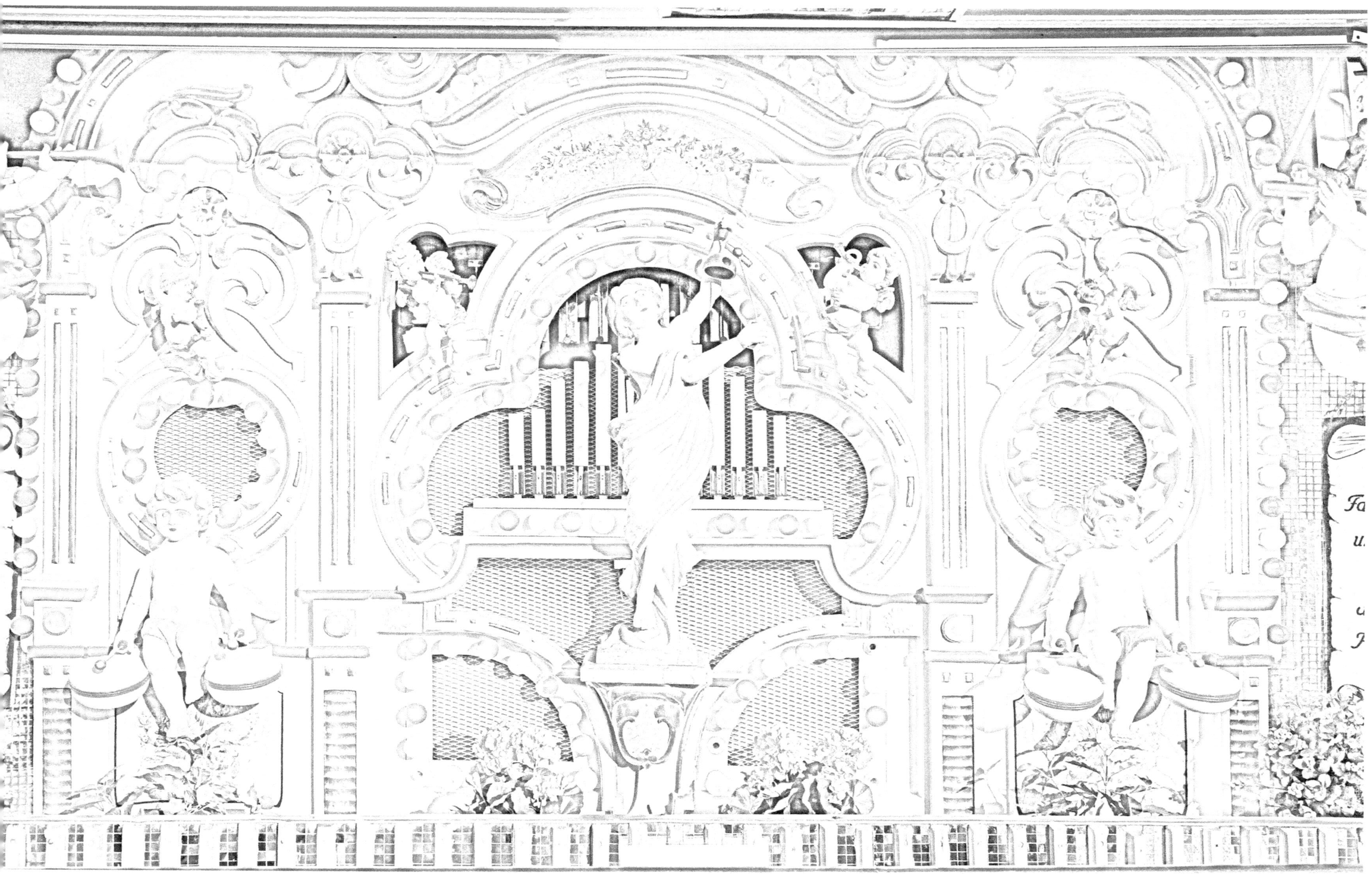

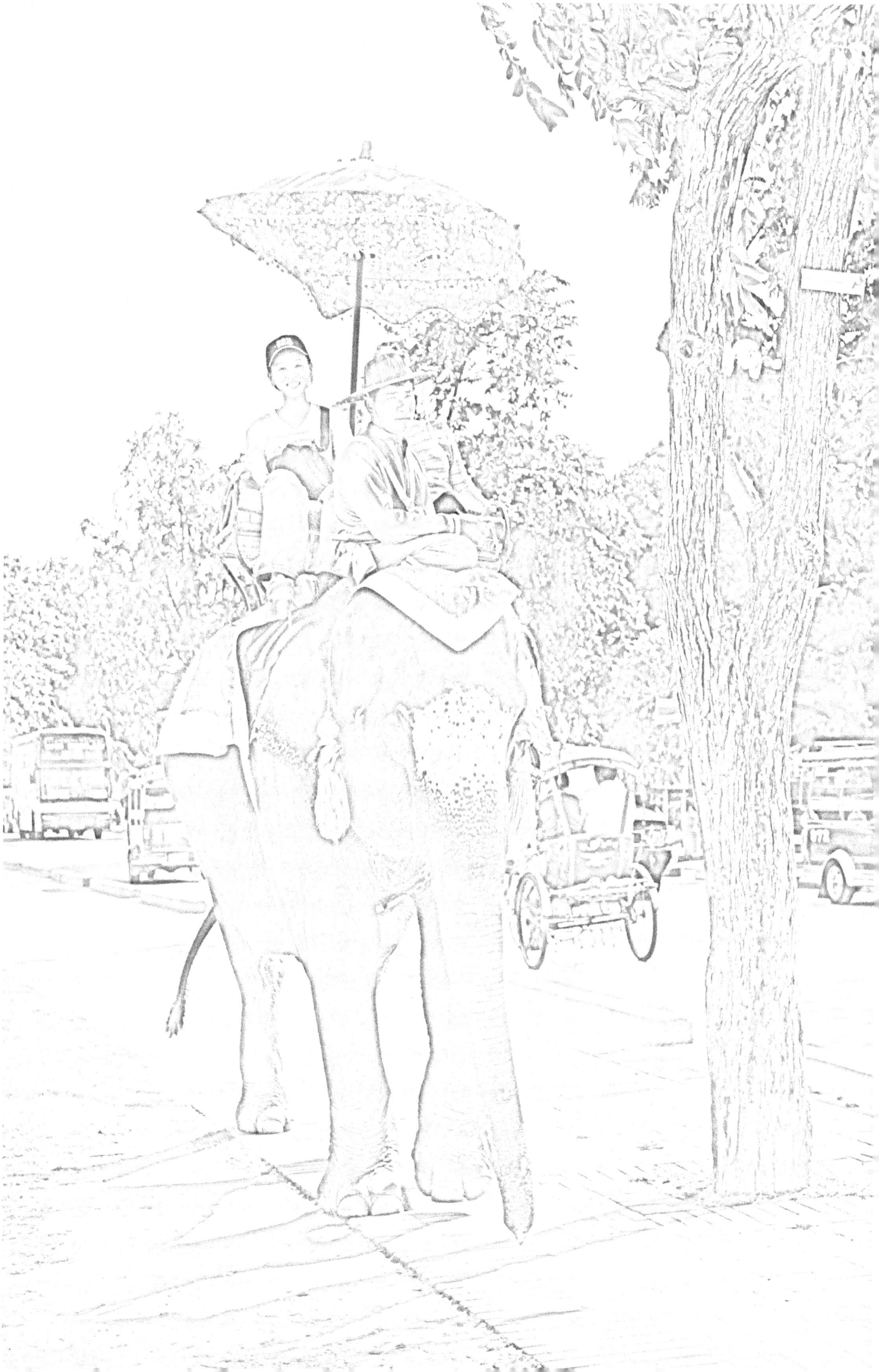

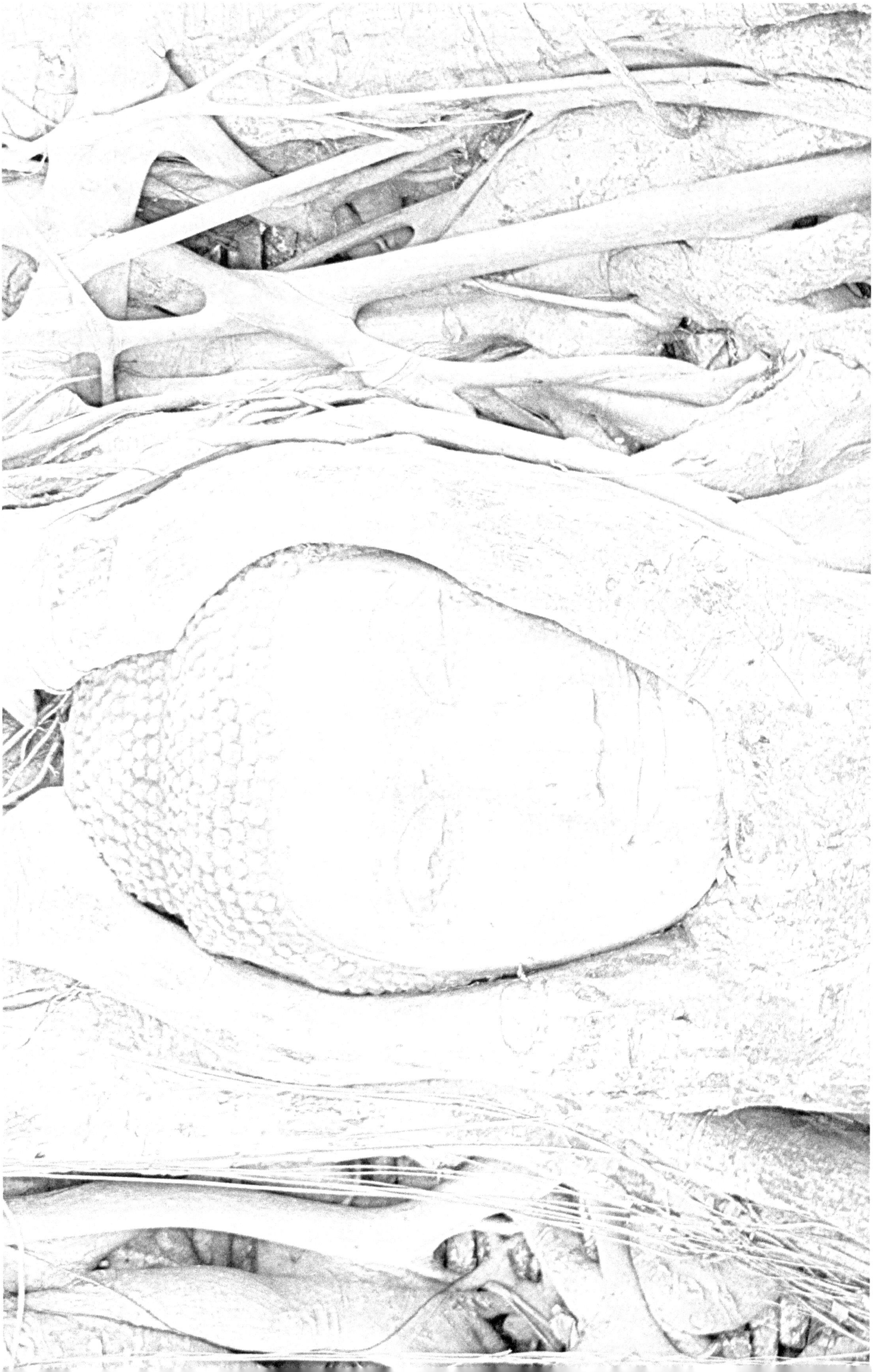

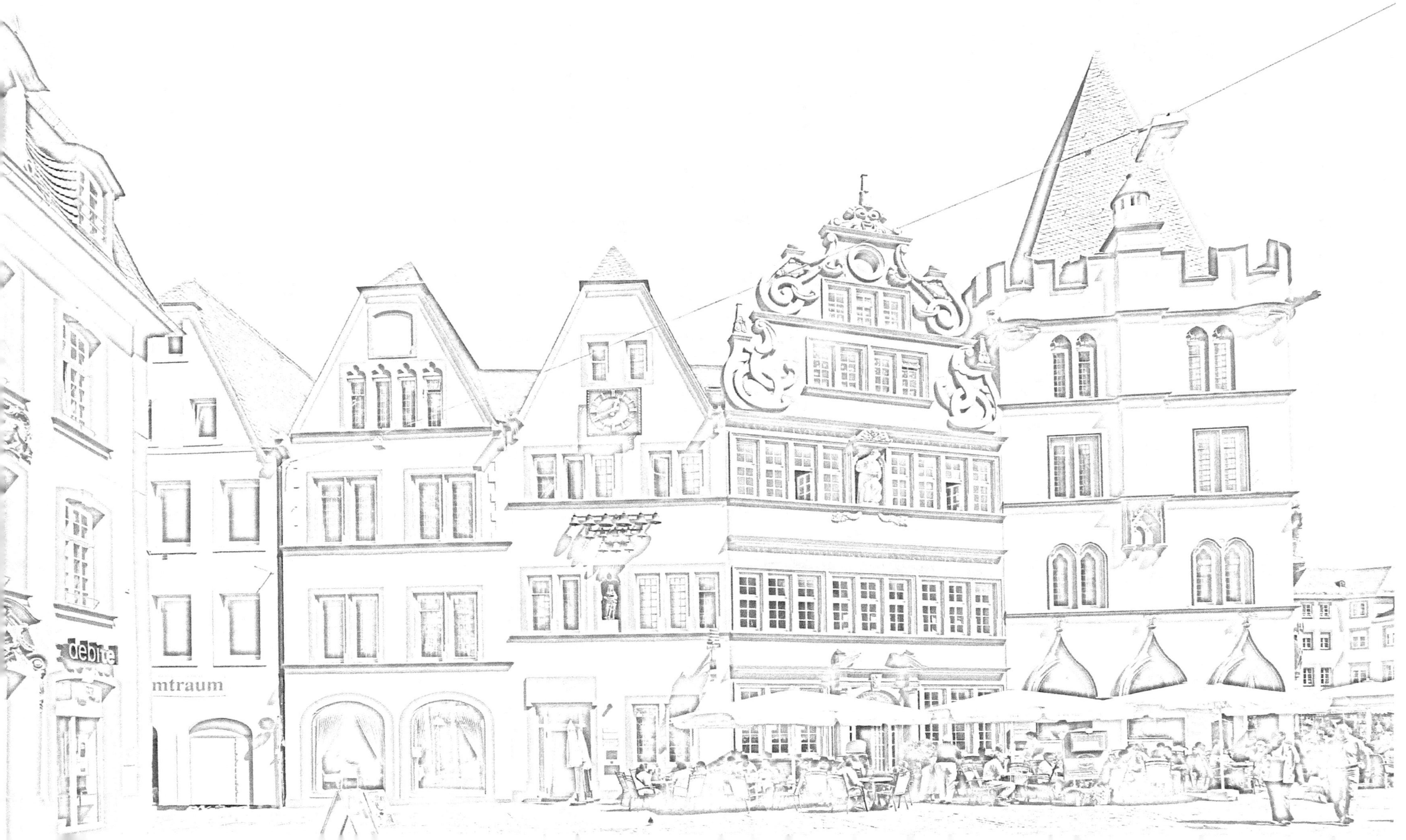
debite
mtraum

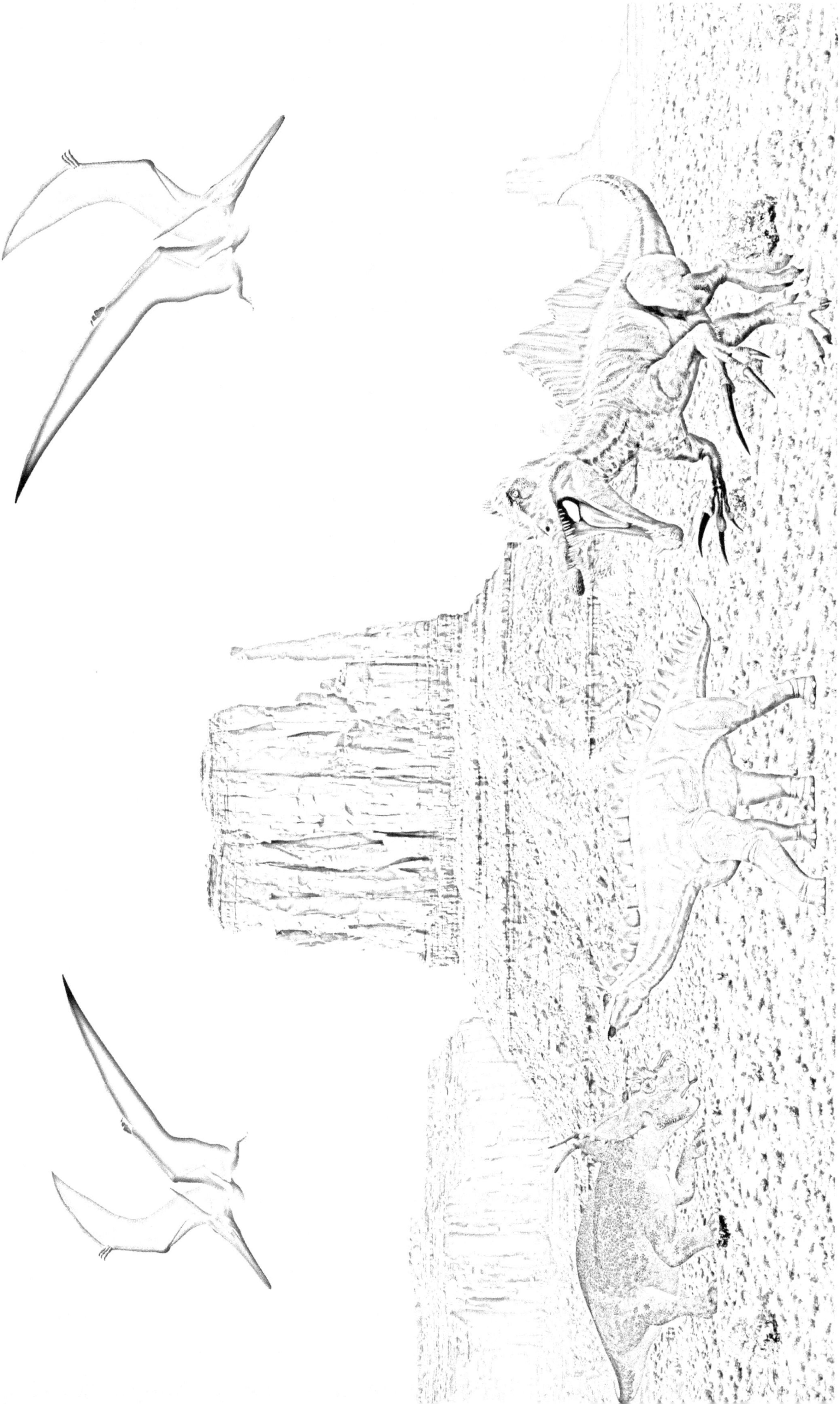

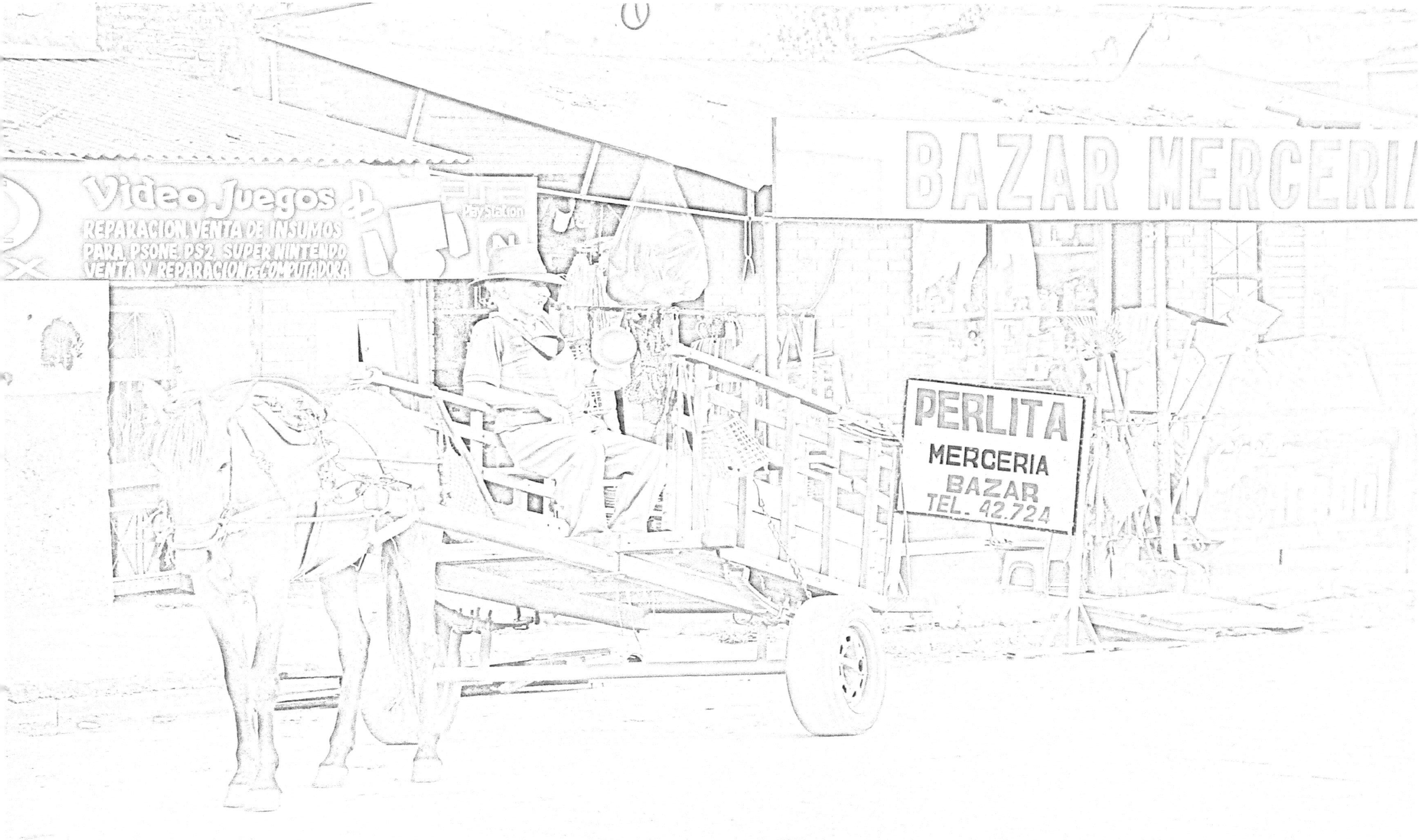
Video Juegos
REPARACION VENTA DE INSUMOS
PARA PSONE PS2 SUPER NINTENDO
VENTA Y REPARACION DE COMPUTADORA
BAZAR MERCERIA
PERLITA
MERCERIA
BAZAR
TEL. 42.724

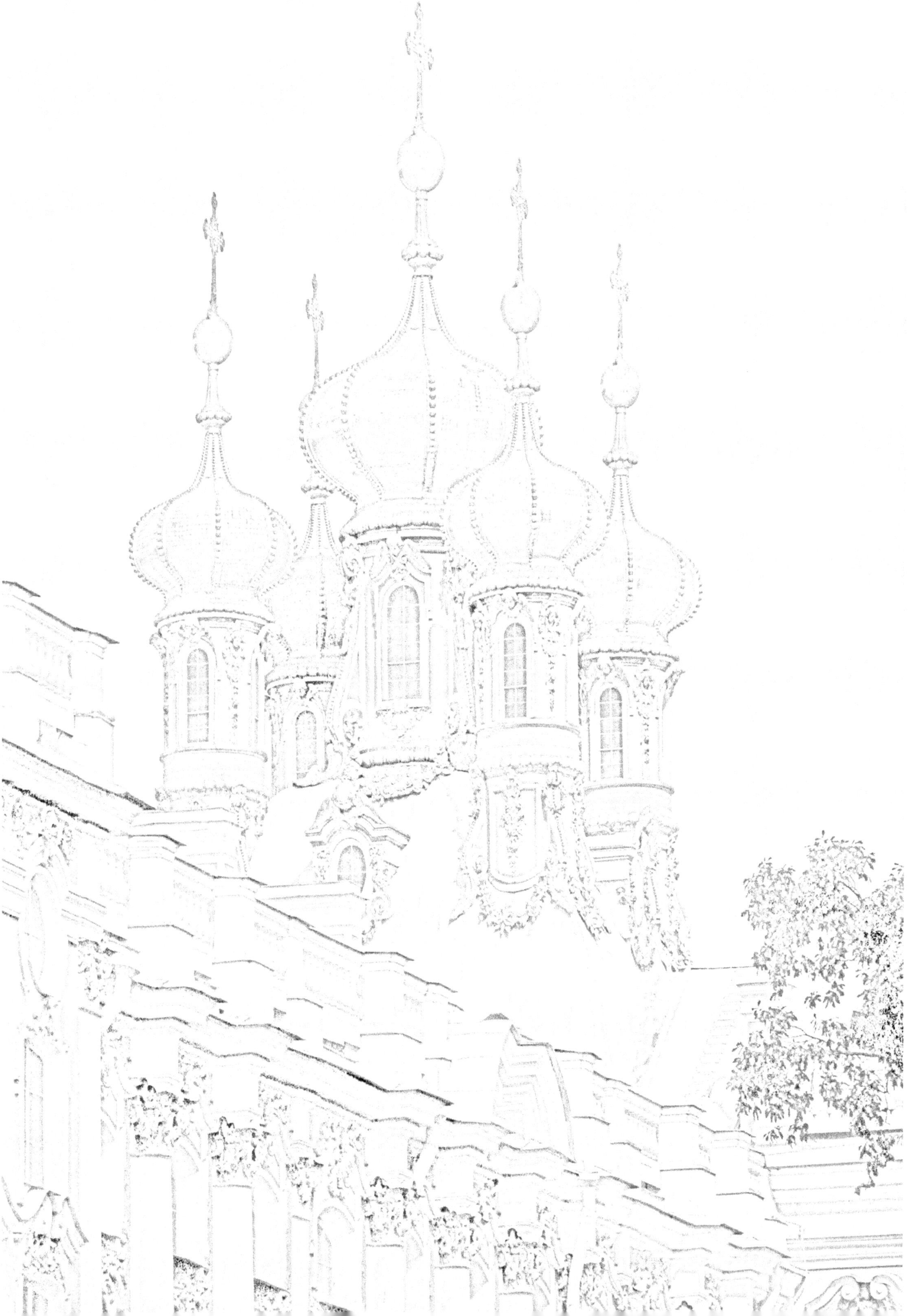

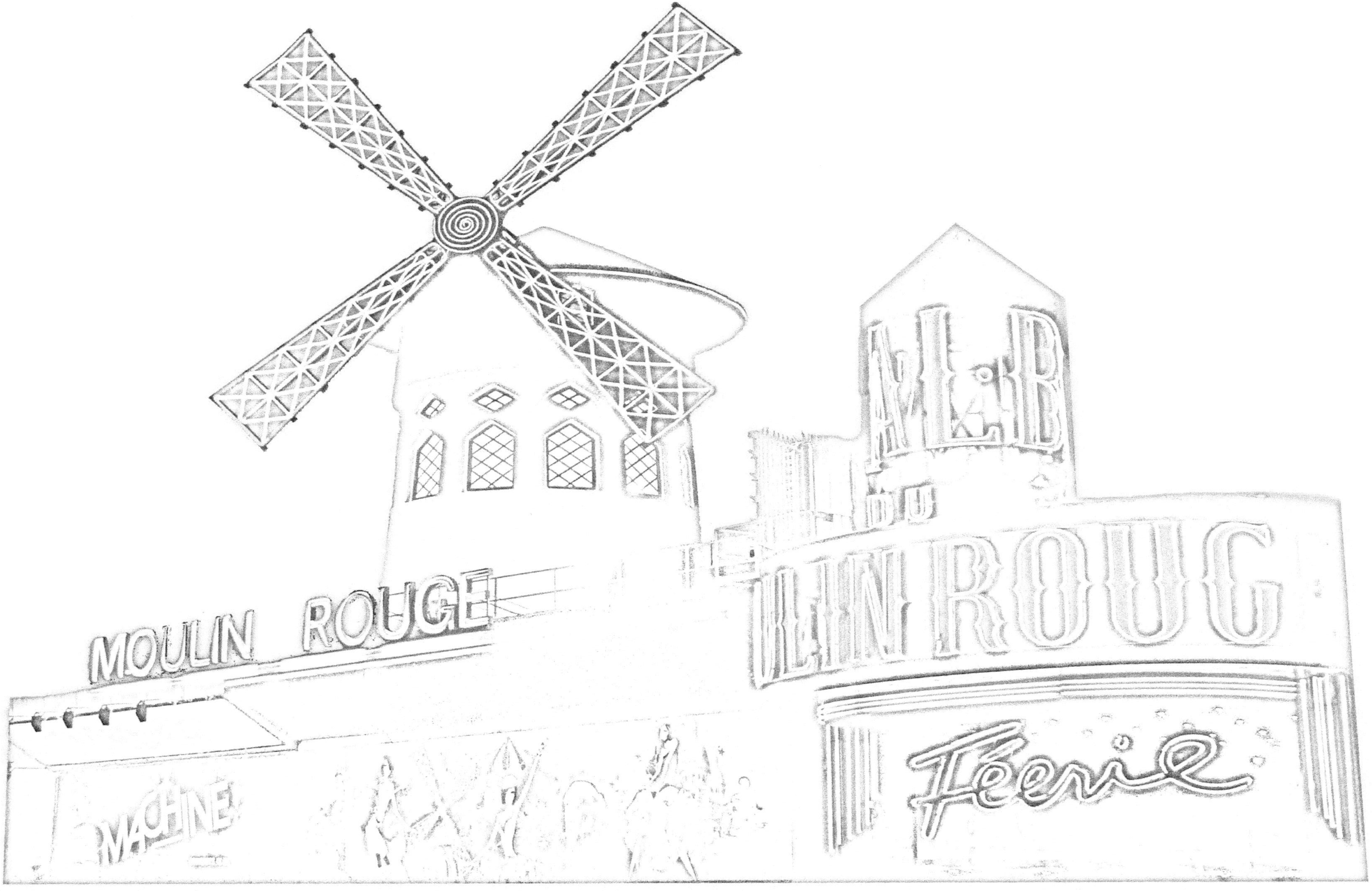
MOULIN ROUGE
BAL
DU
LIN ROUG
Féerie
MACHINE

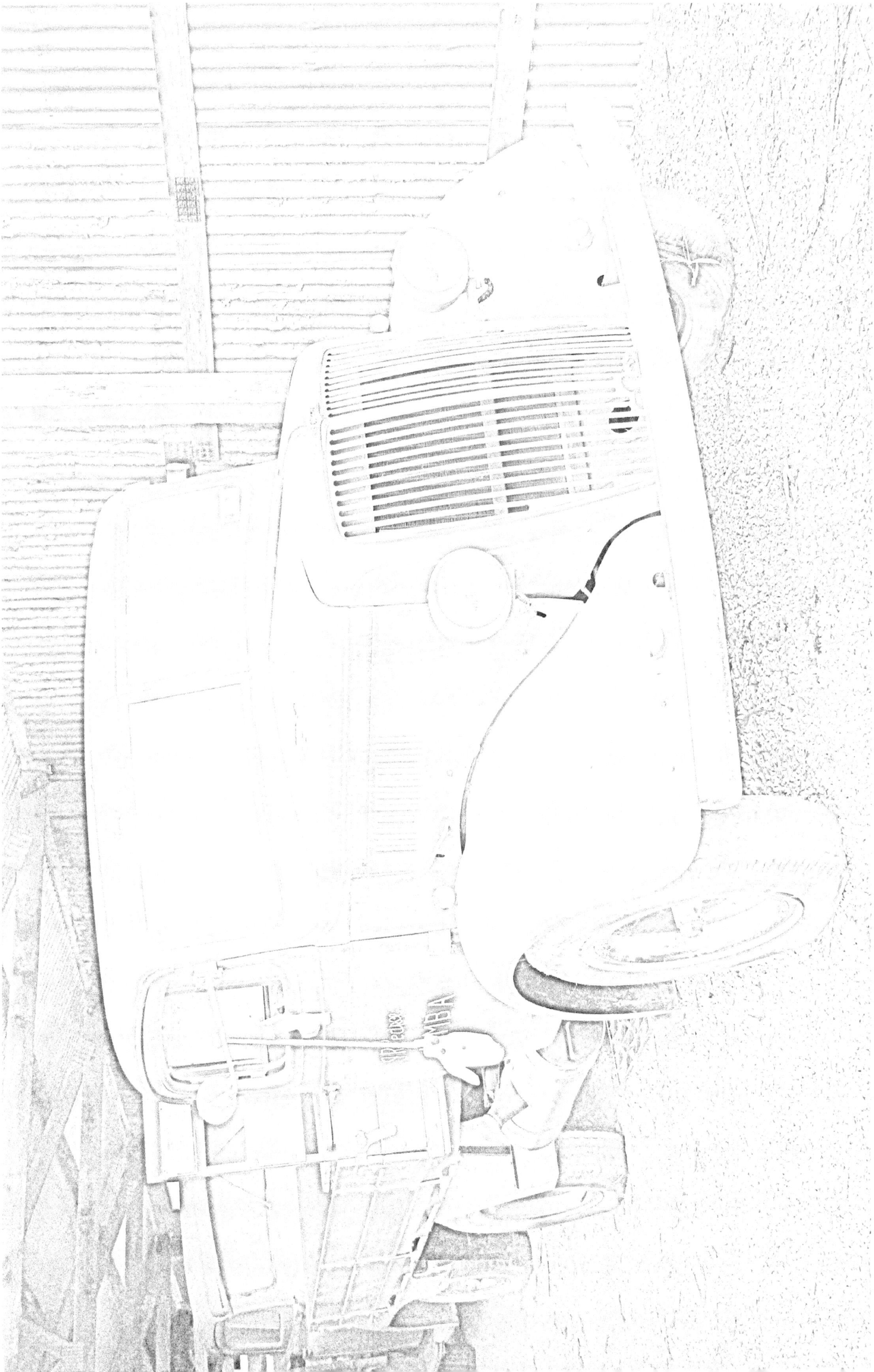

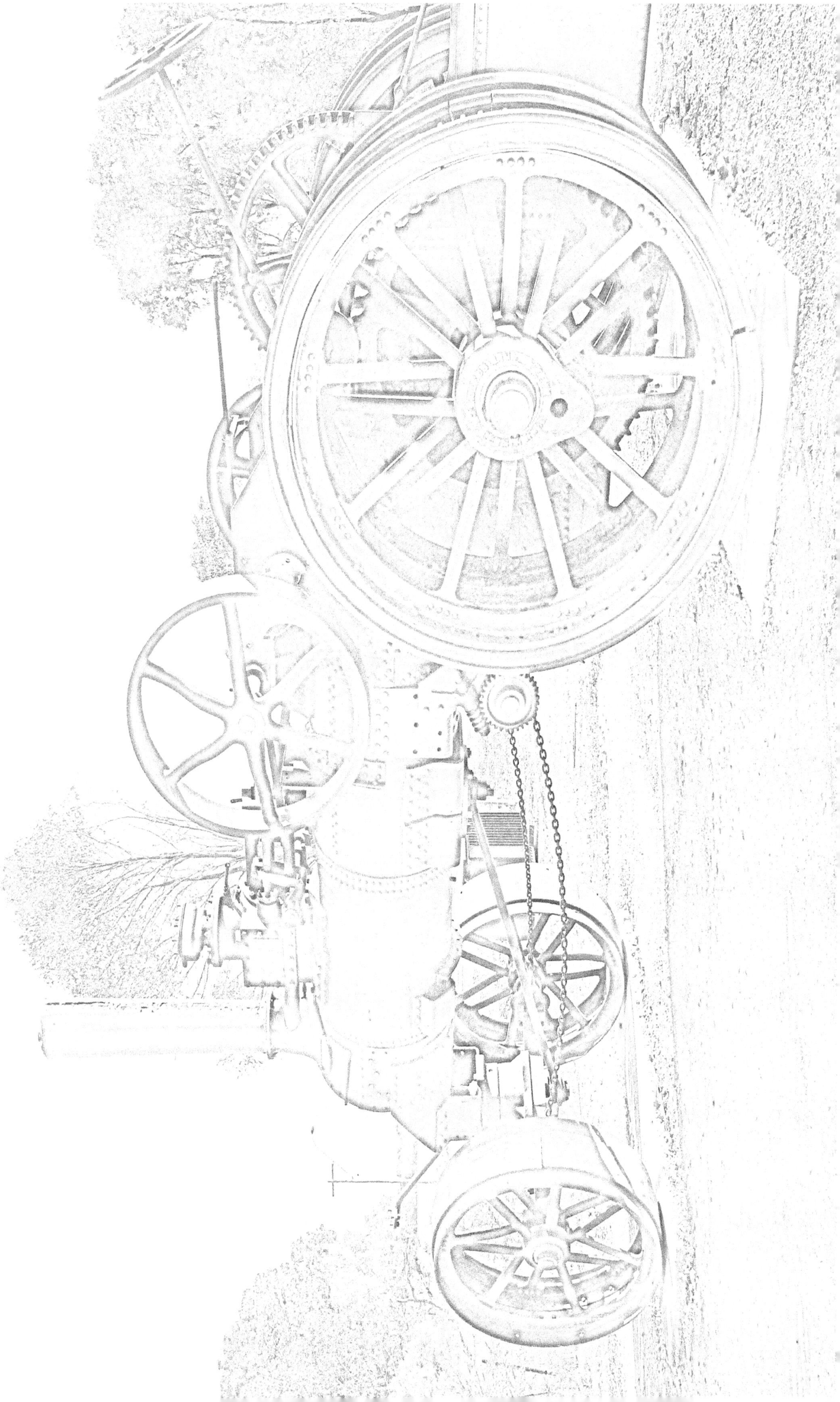

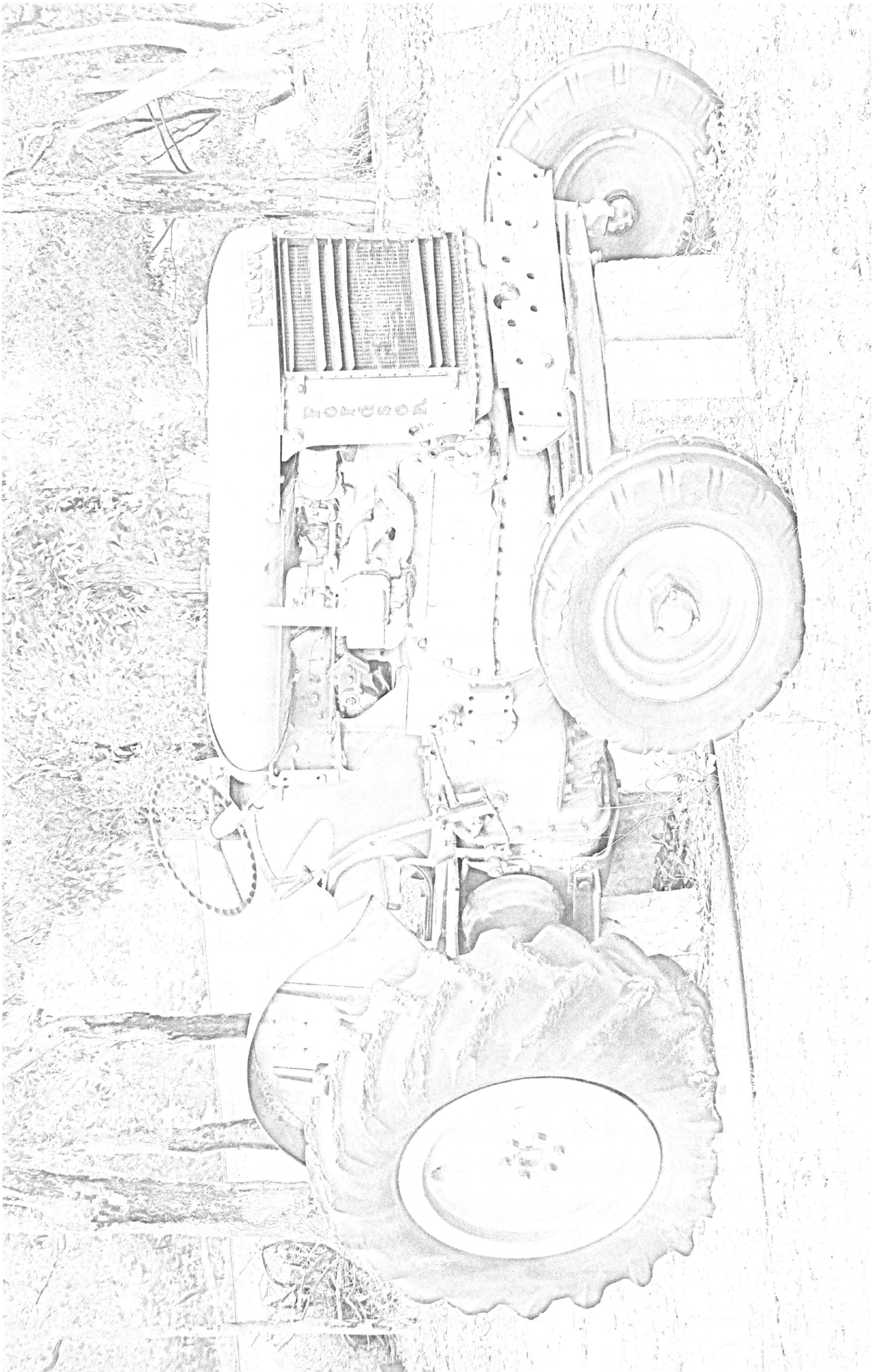

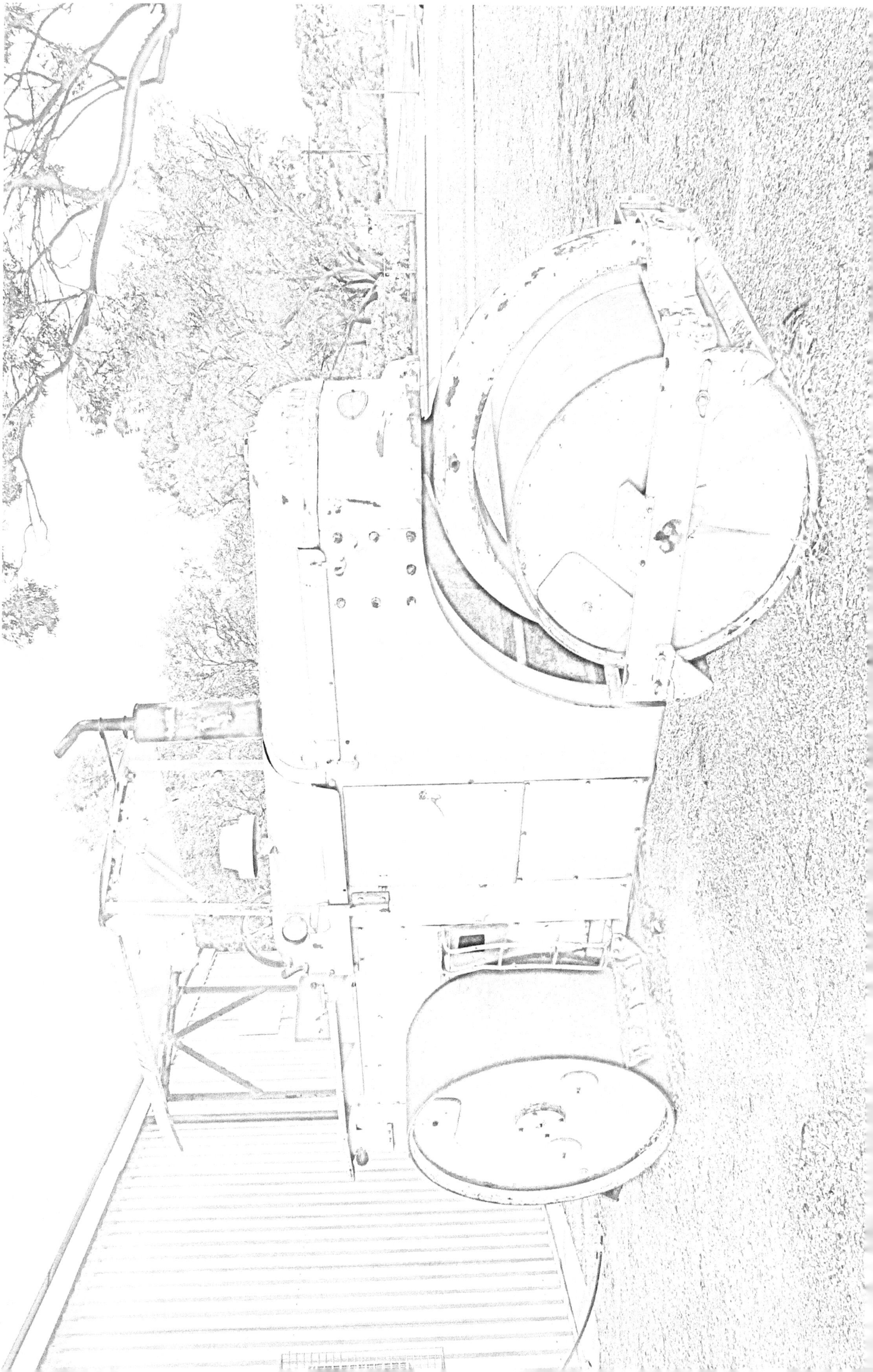

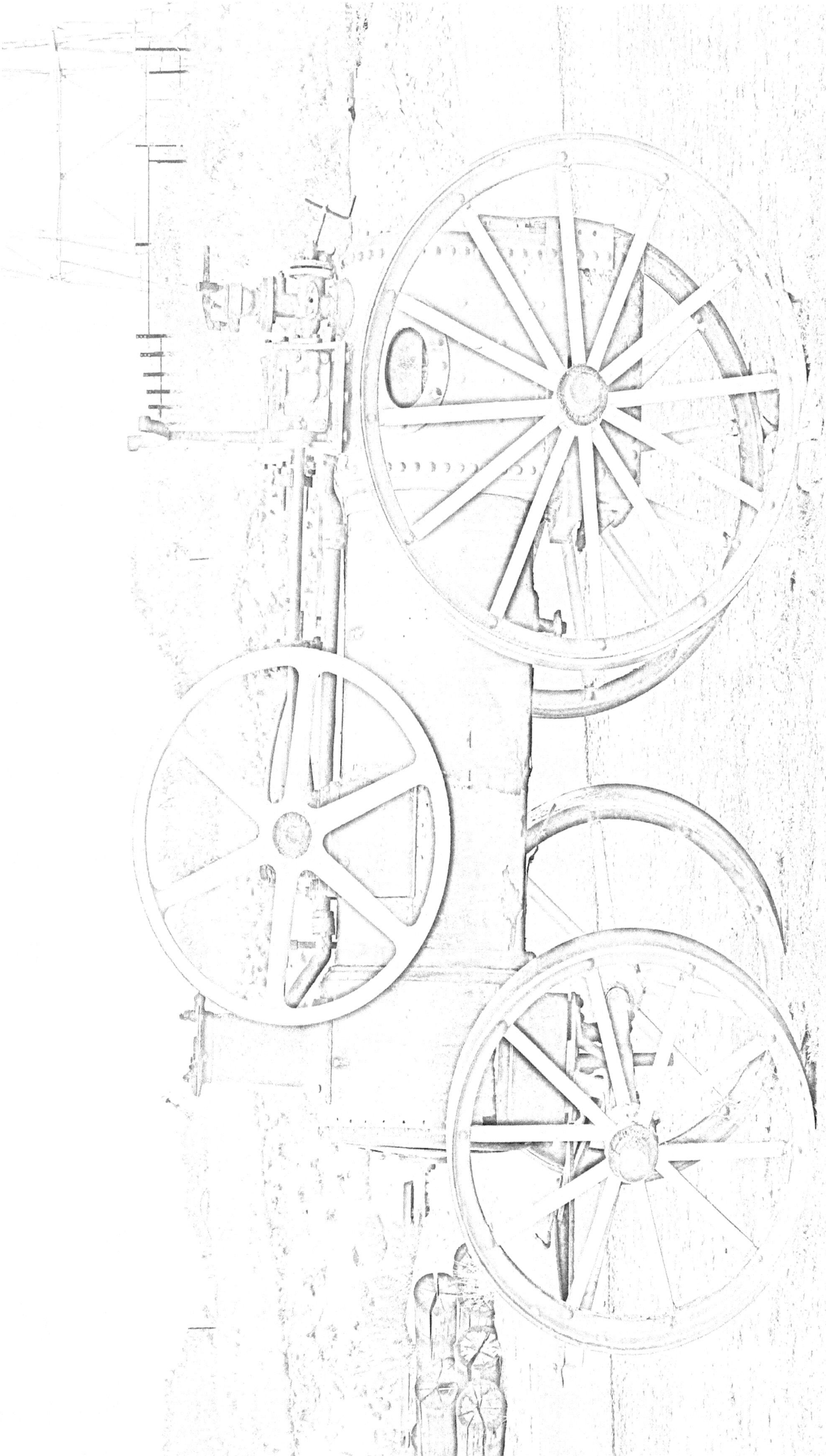

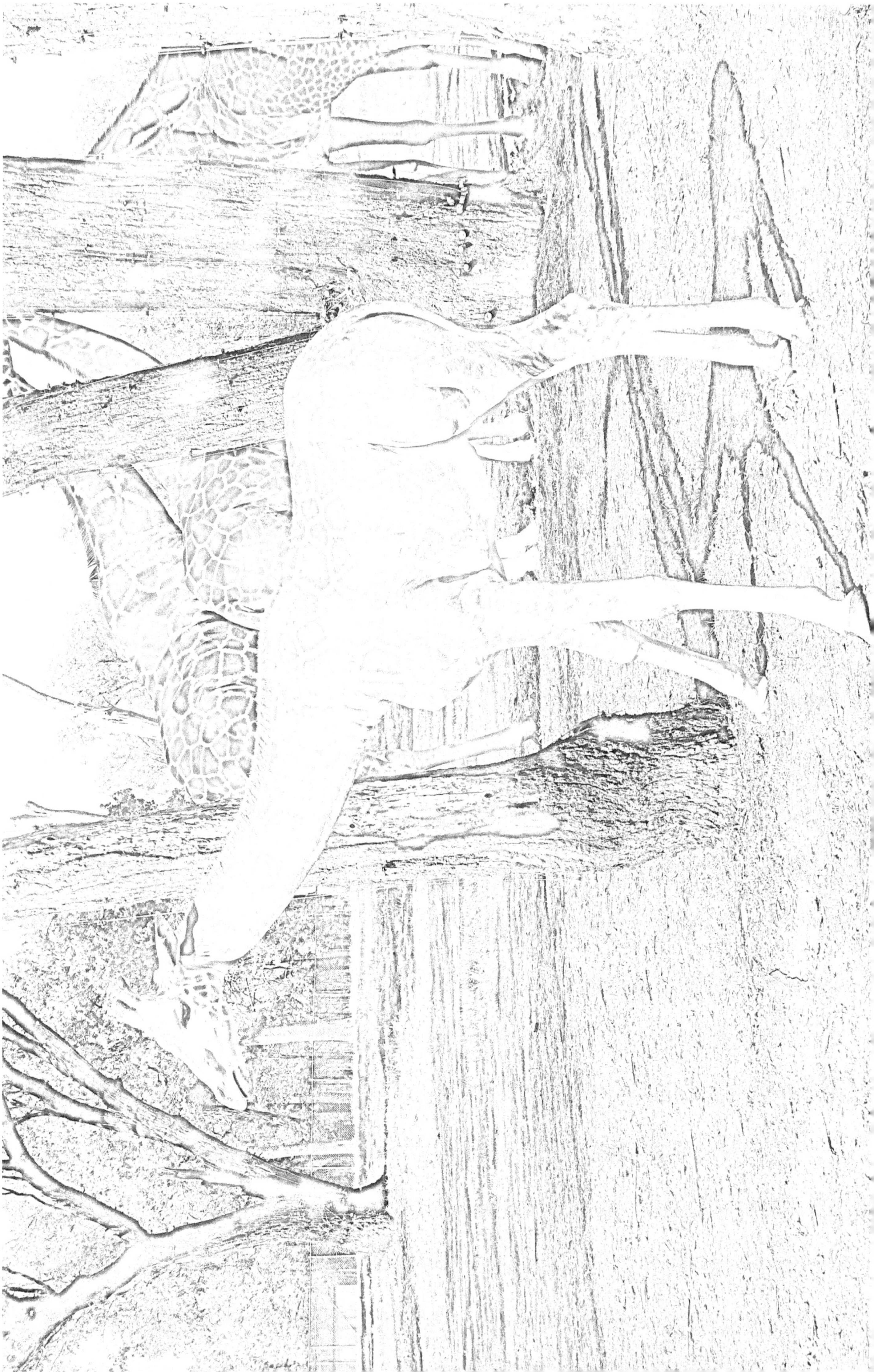

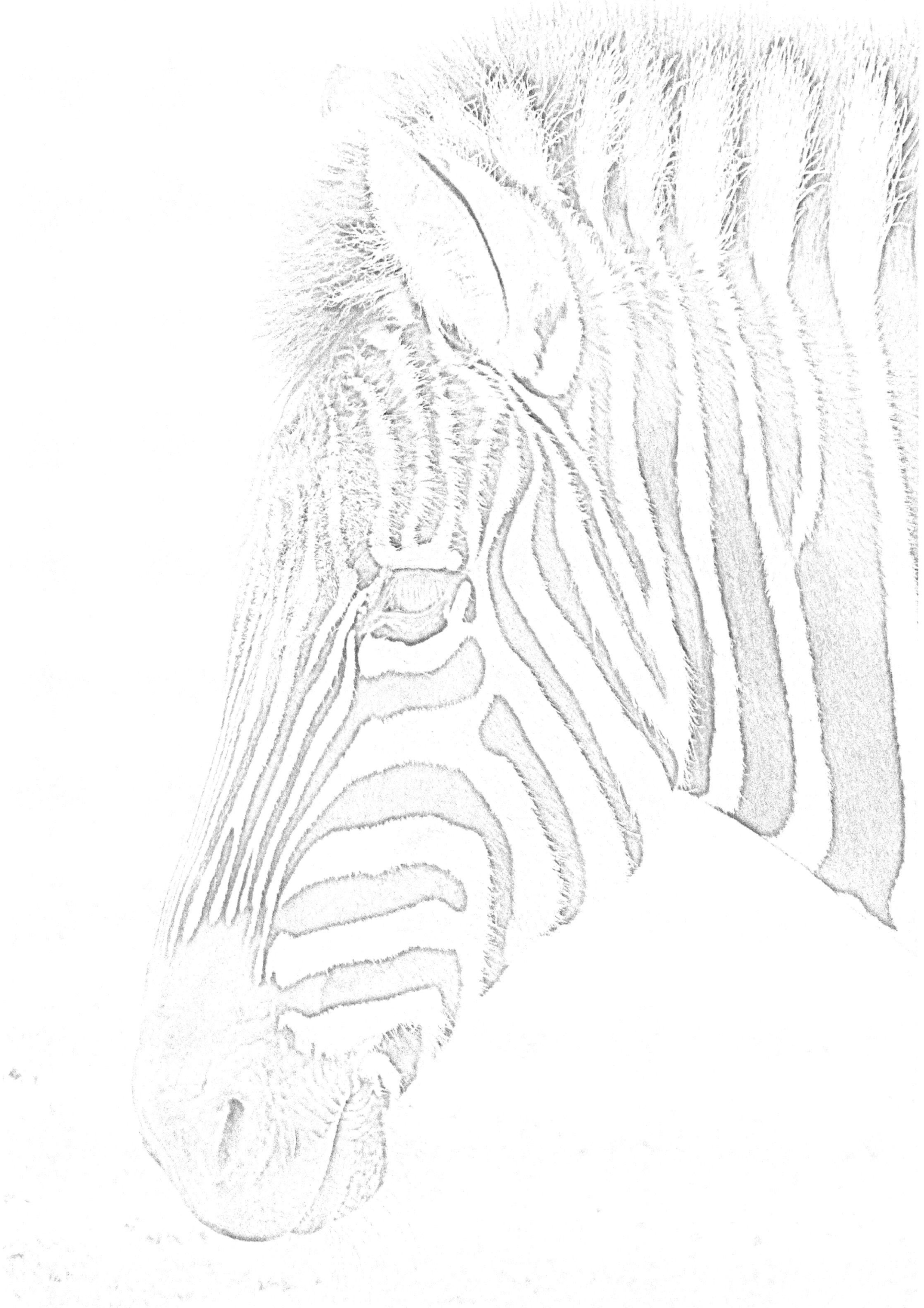

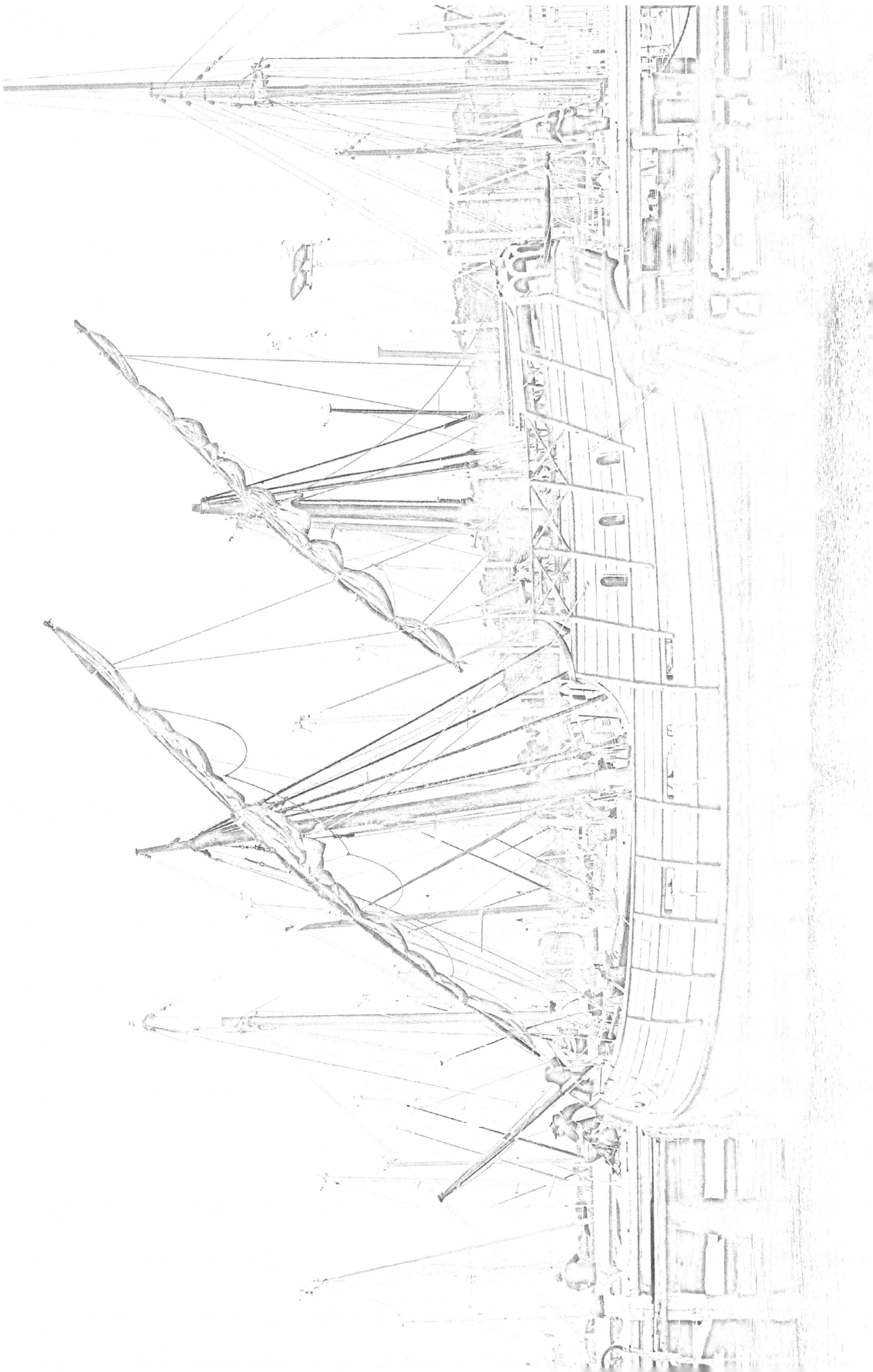

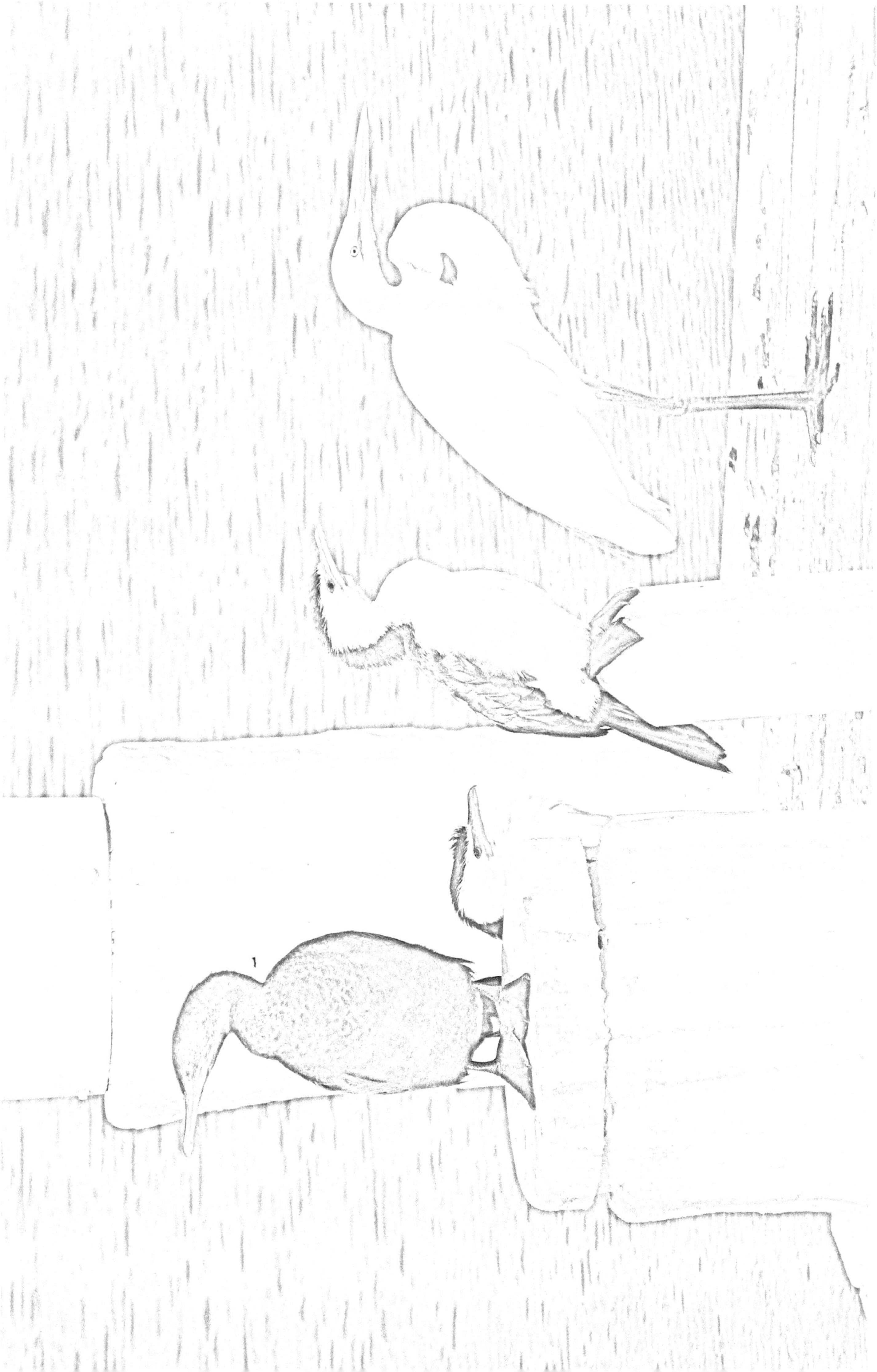

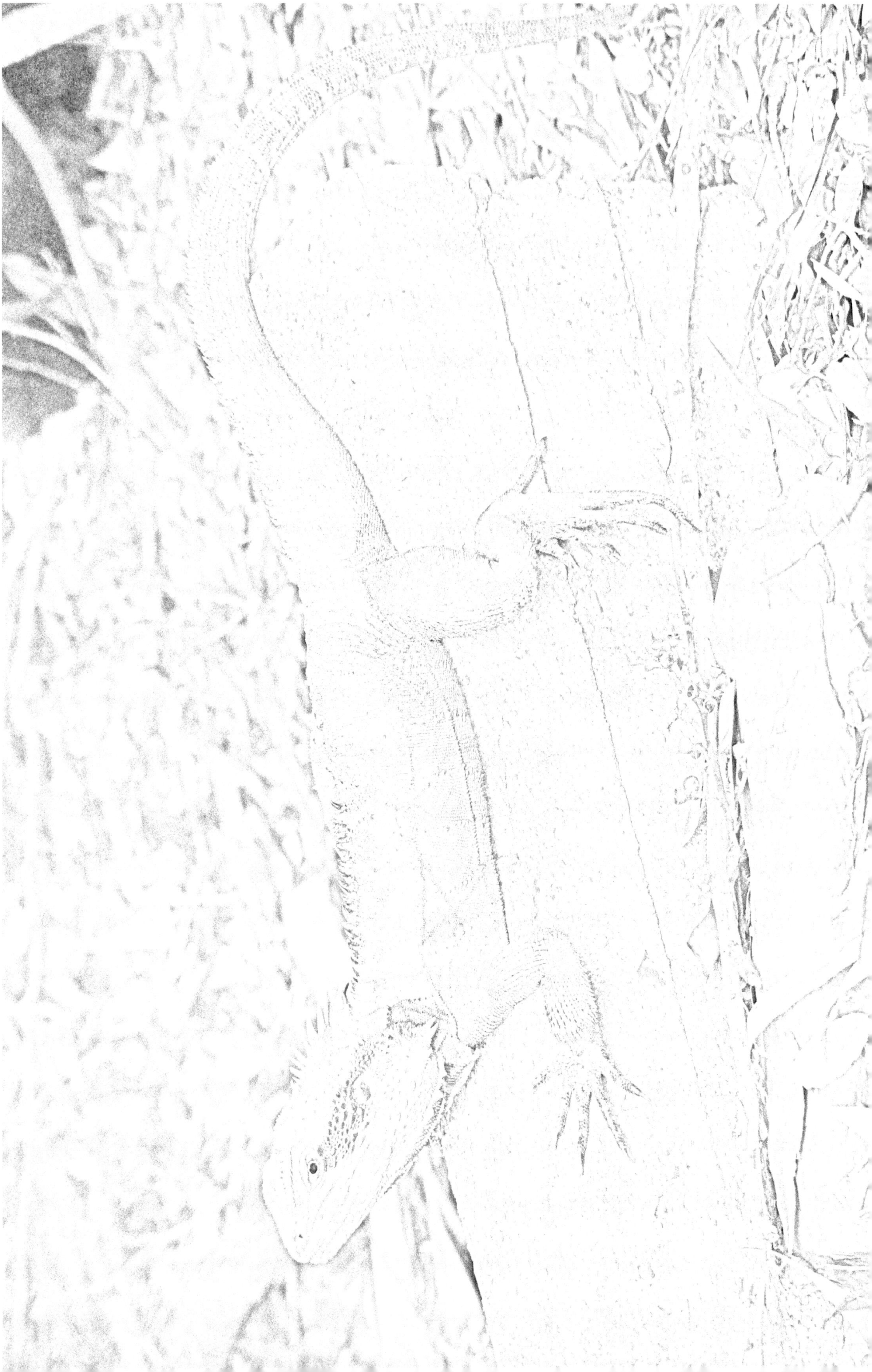

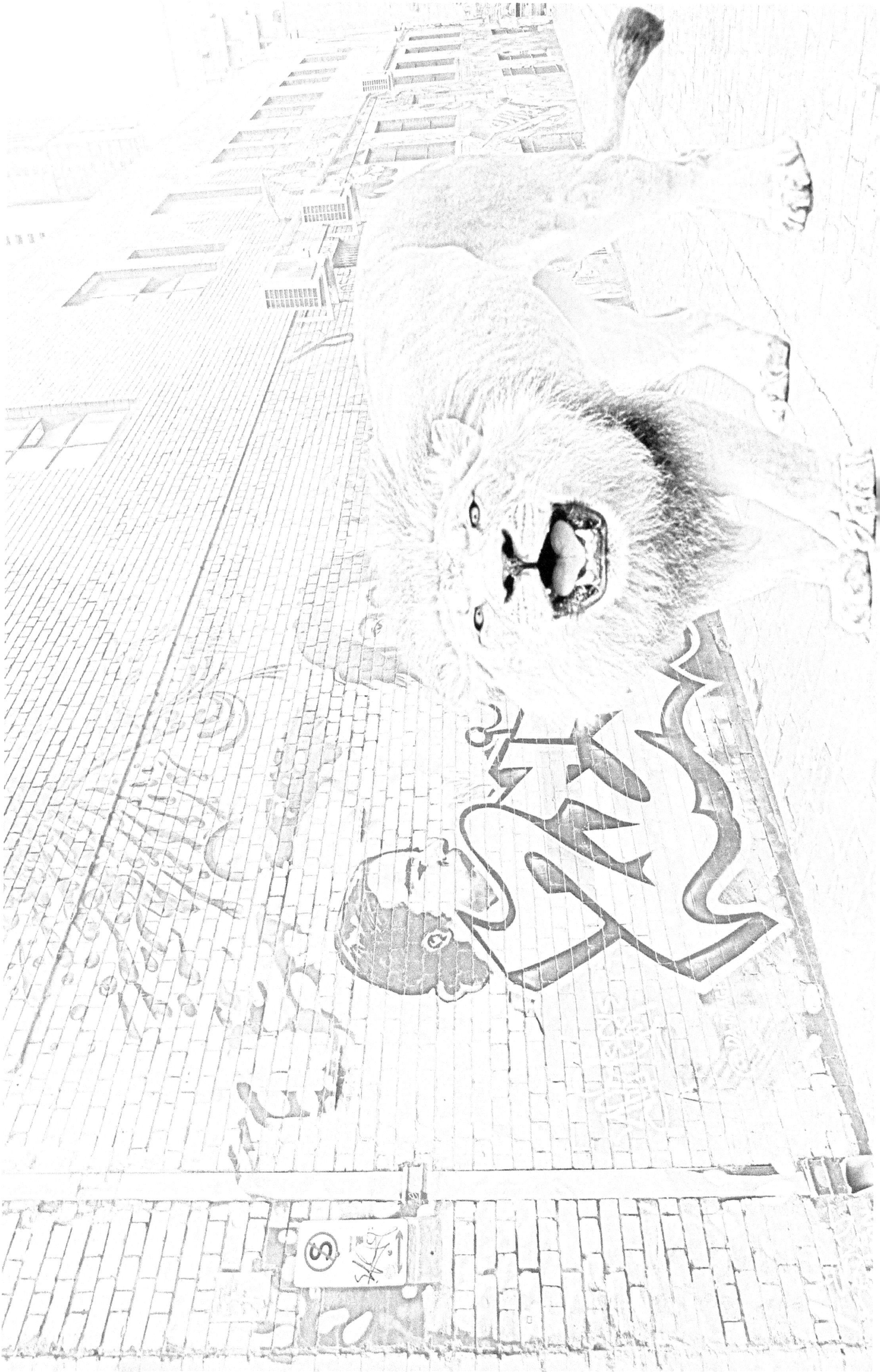

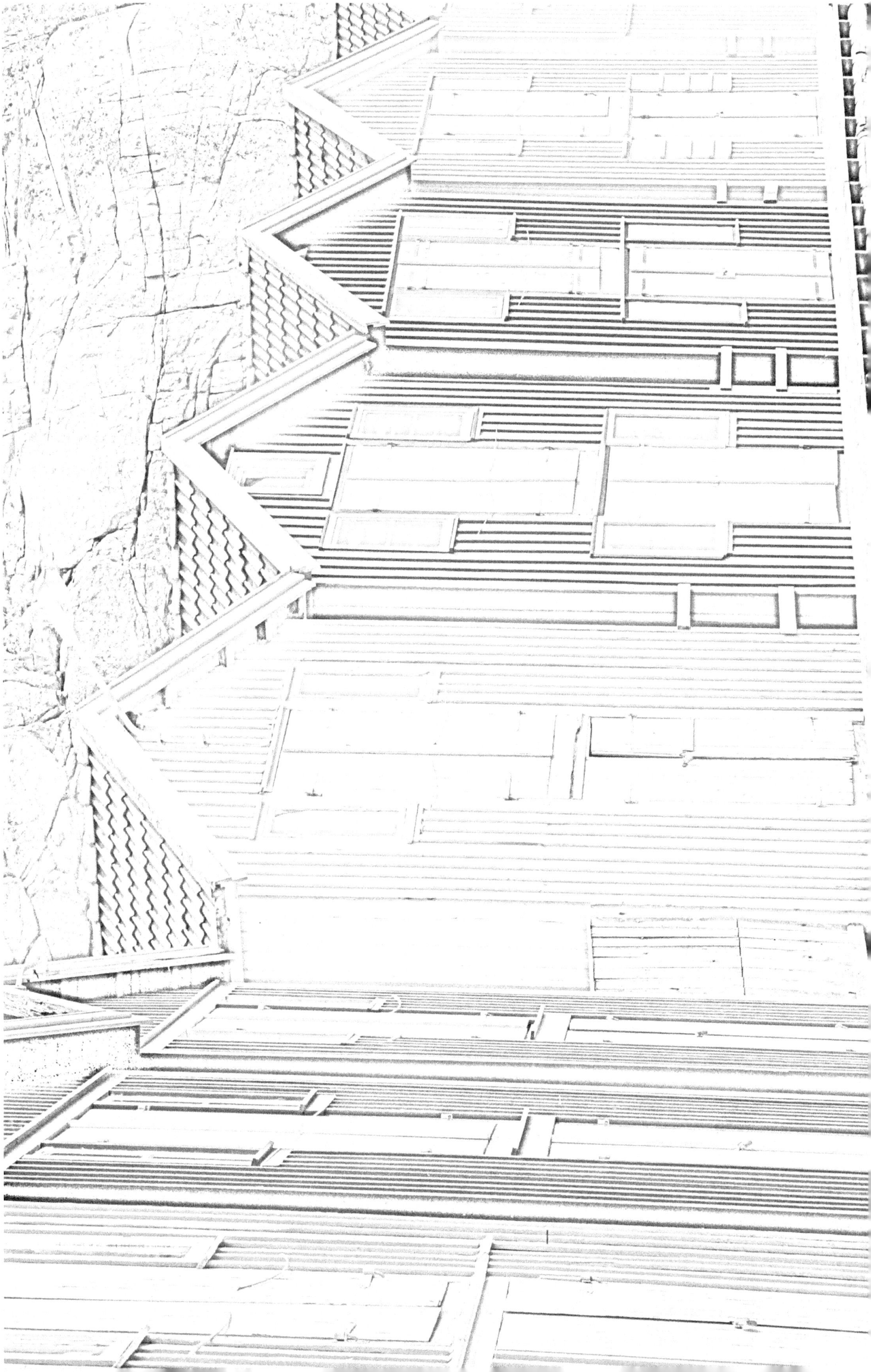

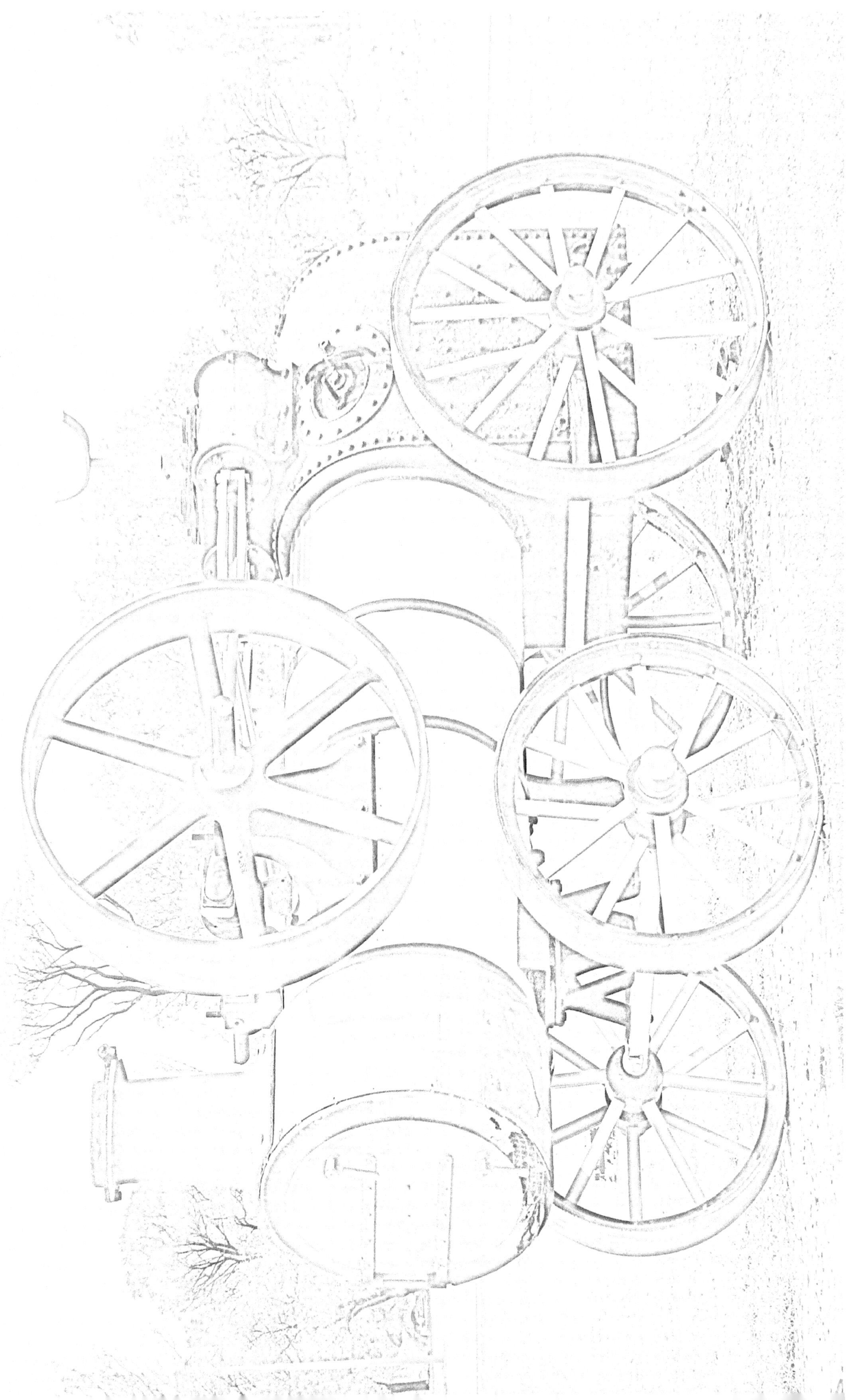

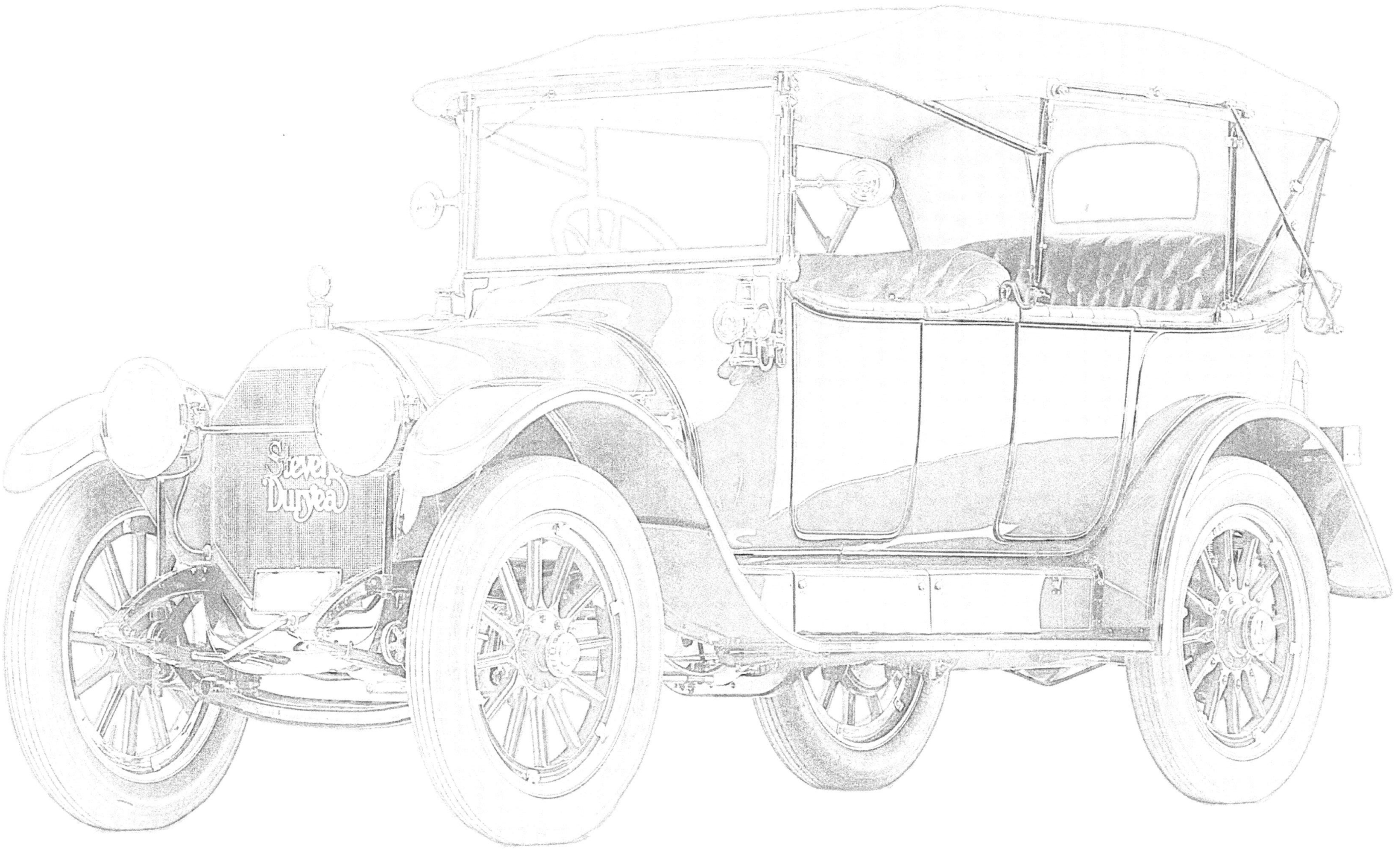
Stevens Duryea

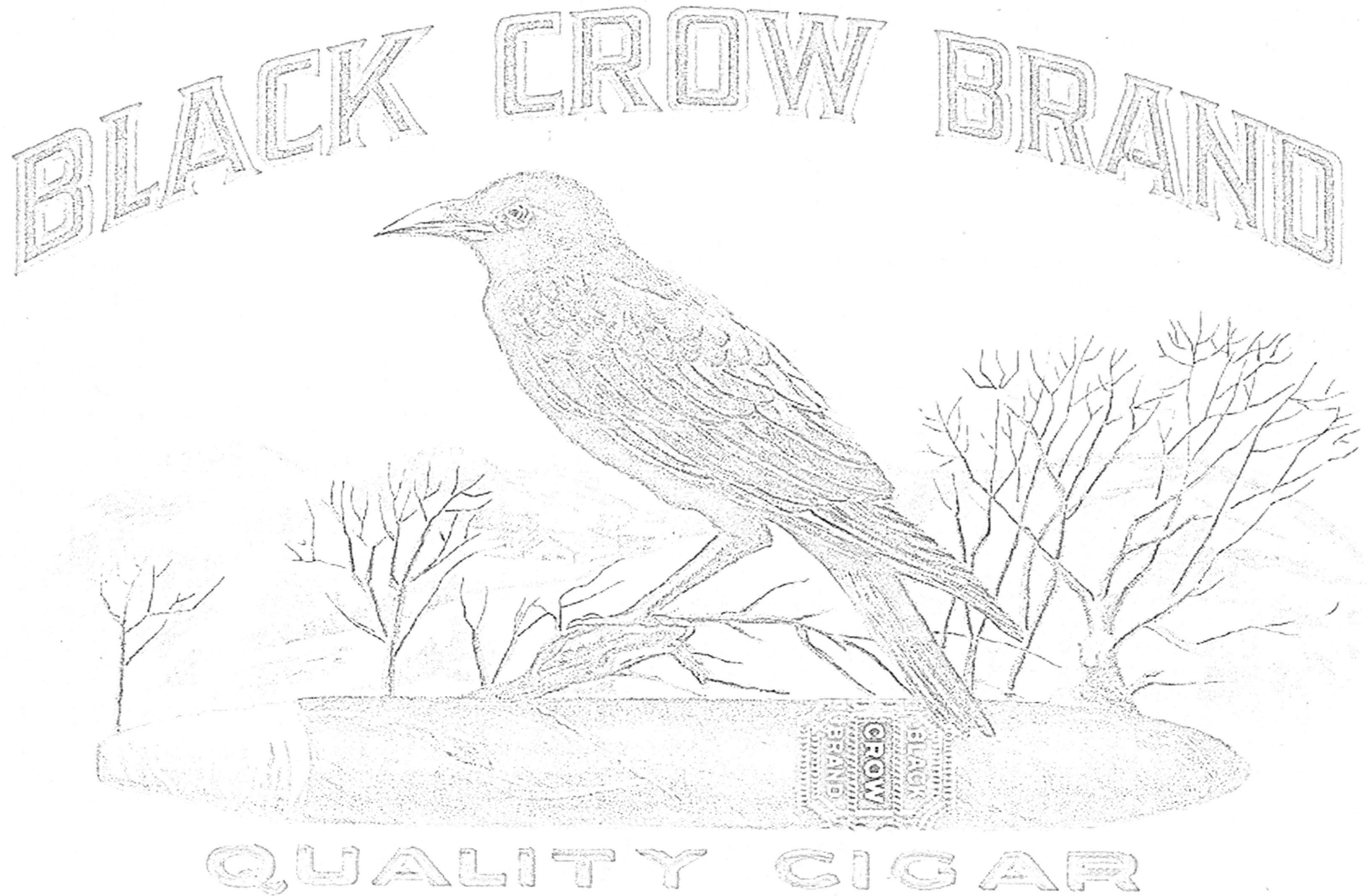
BLACK CROW BRAND
BLACK
CROW
BRAND
QUALITY CIGAR

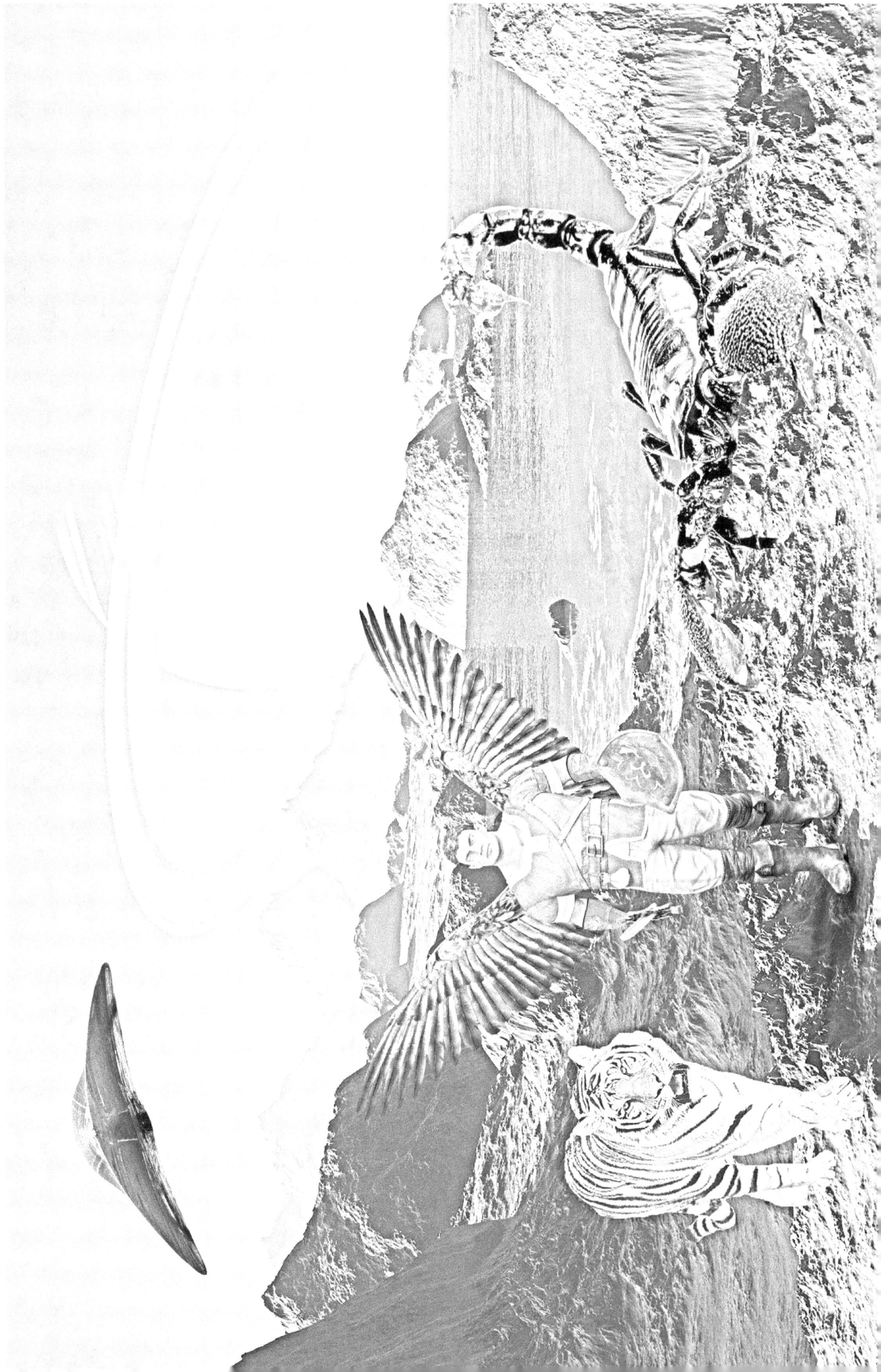

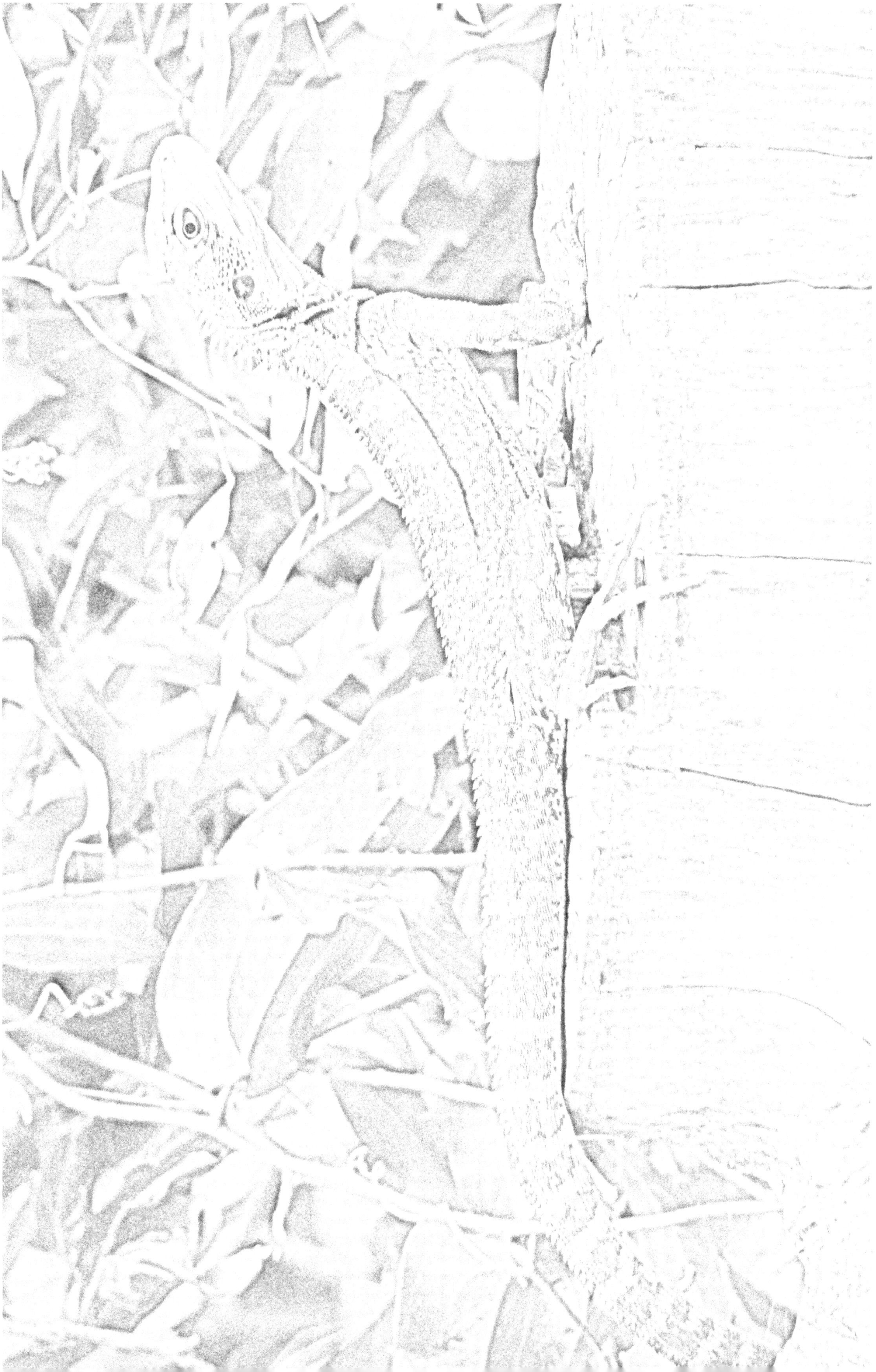

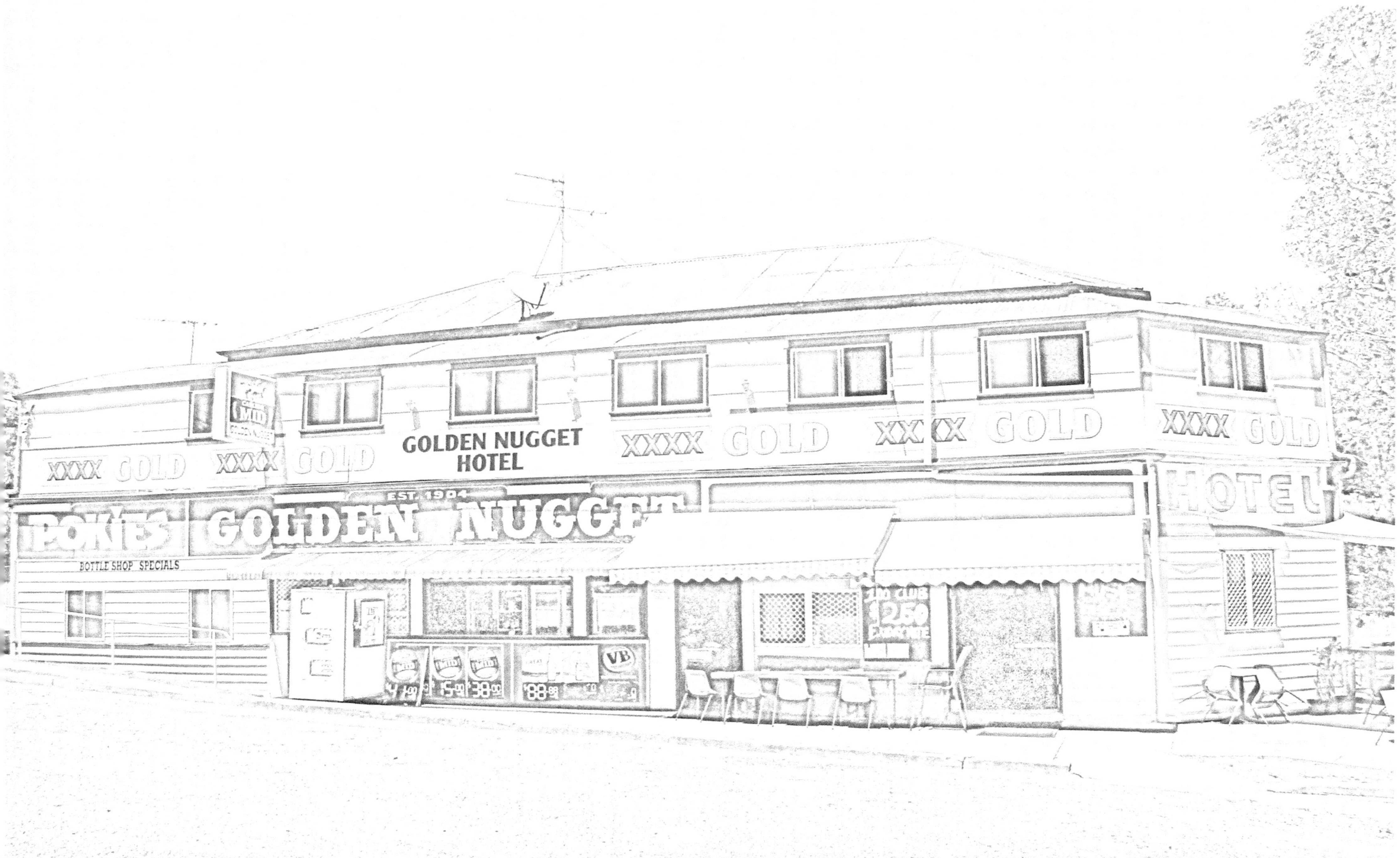
GOLDEN NUGGET
HOTEL
XXXX GOLD
EST. 1904
POKIES
GOLDEN NUGGET
HOTEL
BOTTLE SHOP SPECIALS
VB

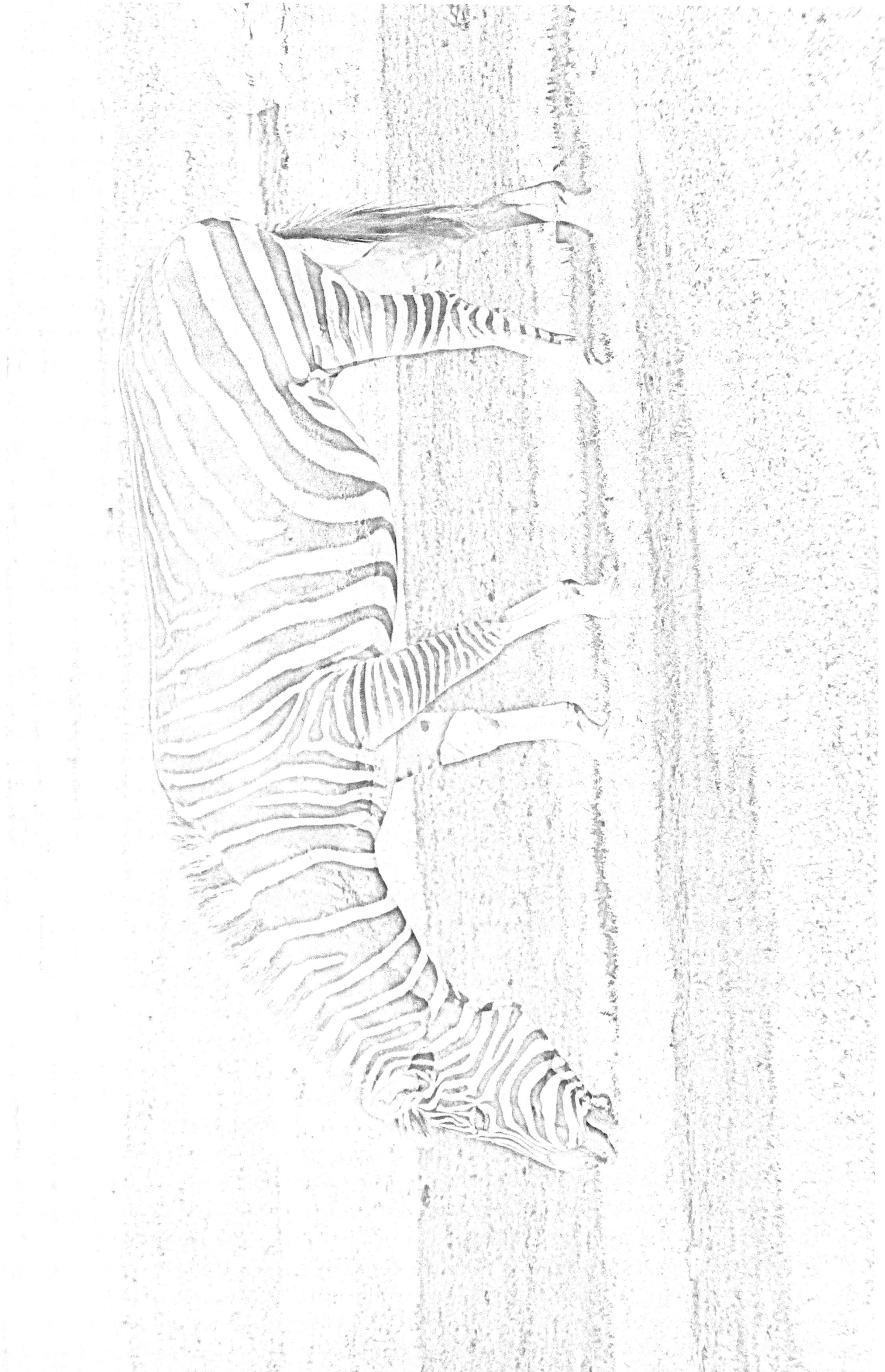

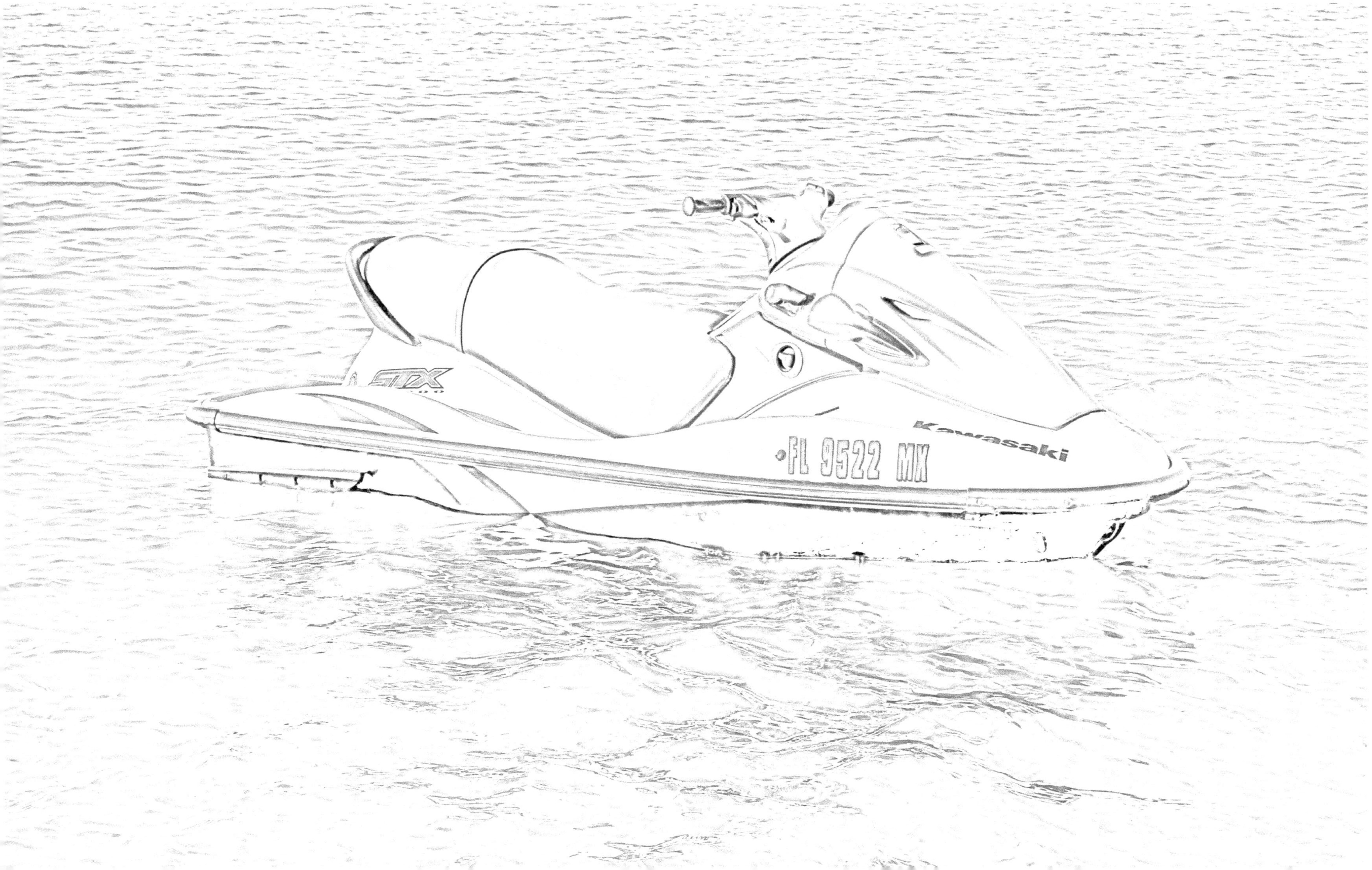
STX
Kawasaki
FL 9522 MX

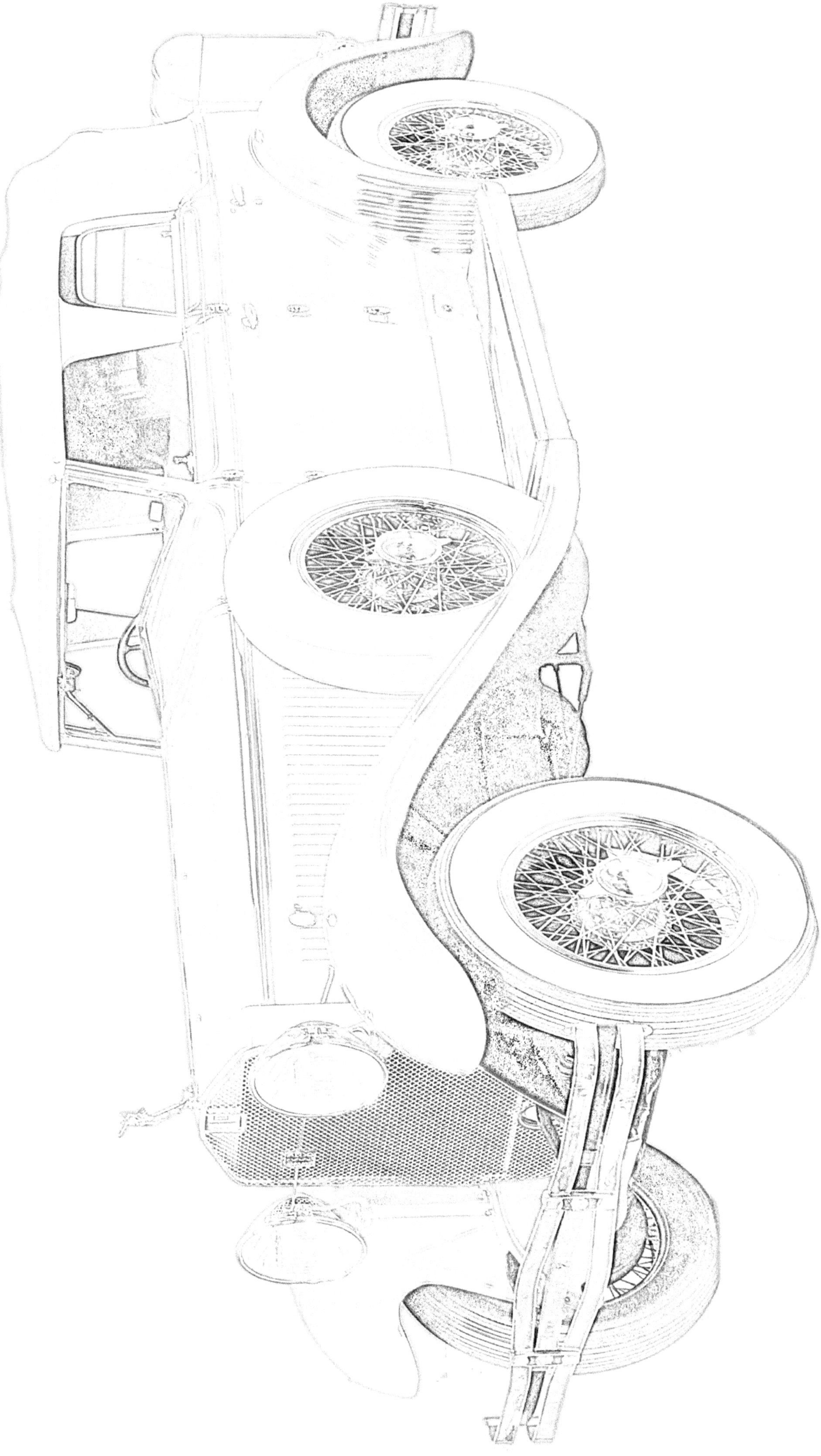

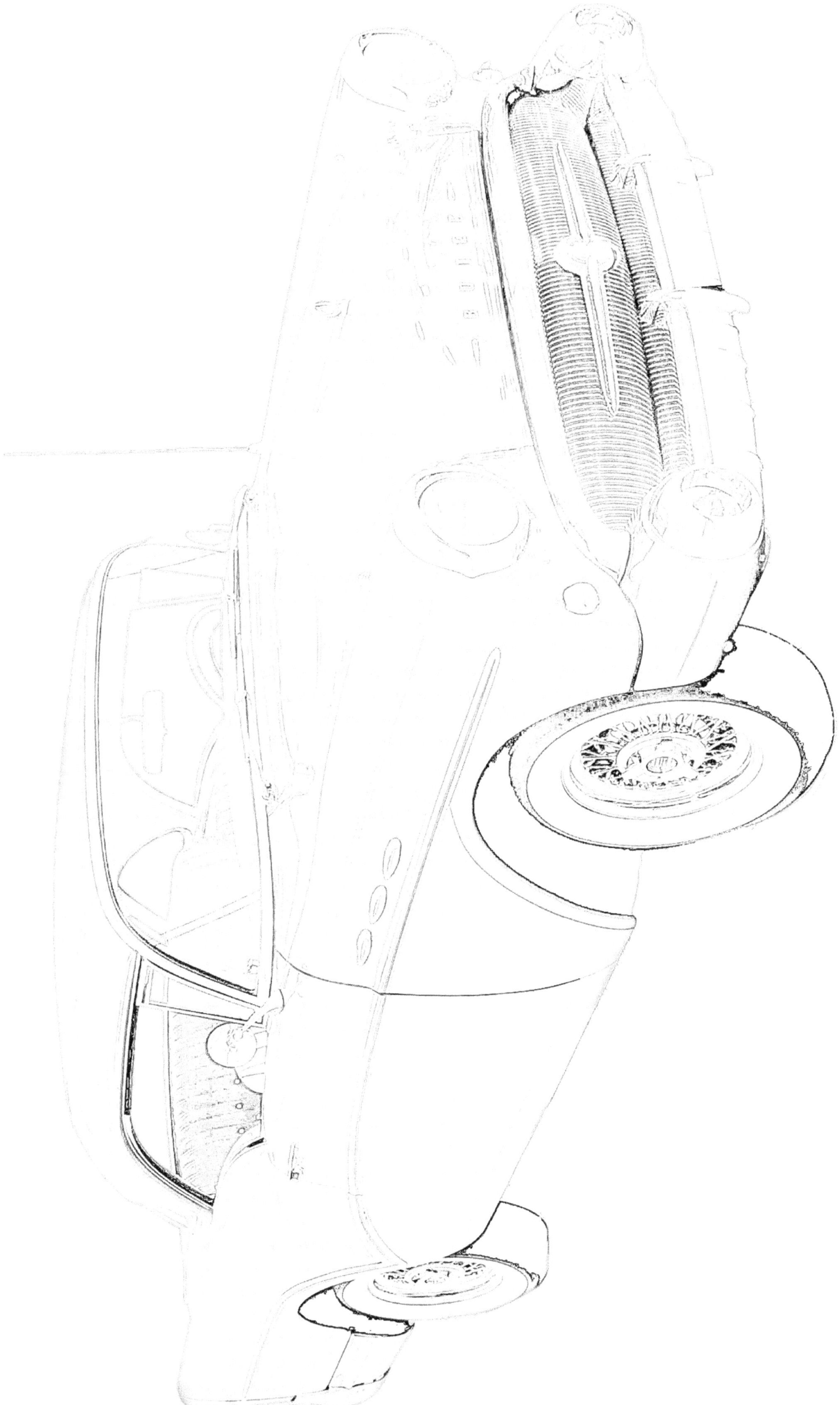

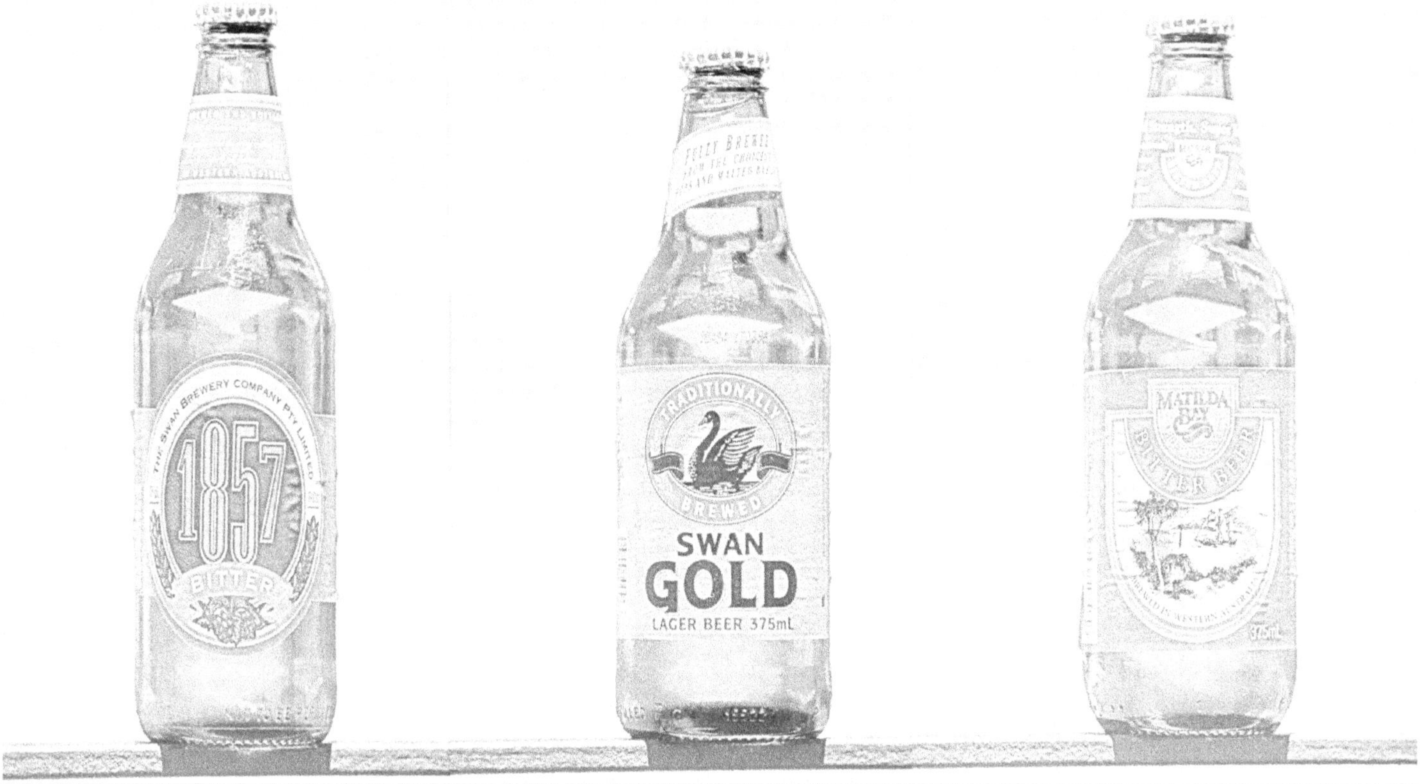
THE SWAN BREWERY COMPANY PTY LIMITED
1857
BITTER
TRADITIONALLY BREWED
SWAN
GOLD
LAGER BEER 375mL
MATILDA BAY
BITTER BEER

Beer

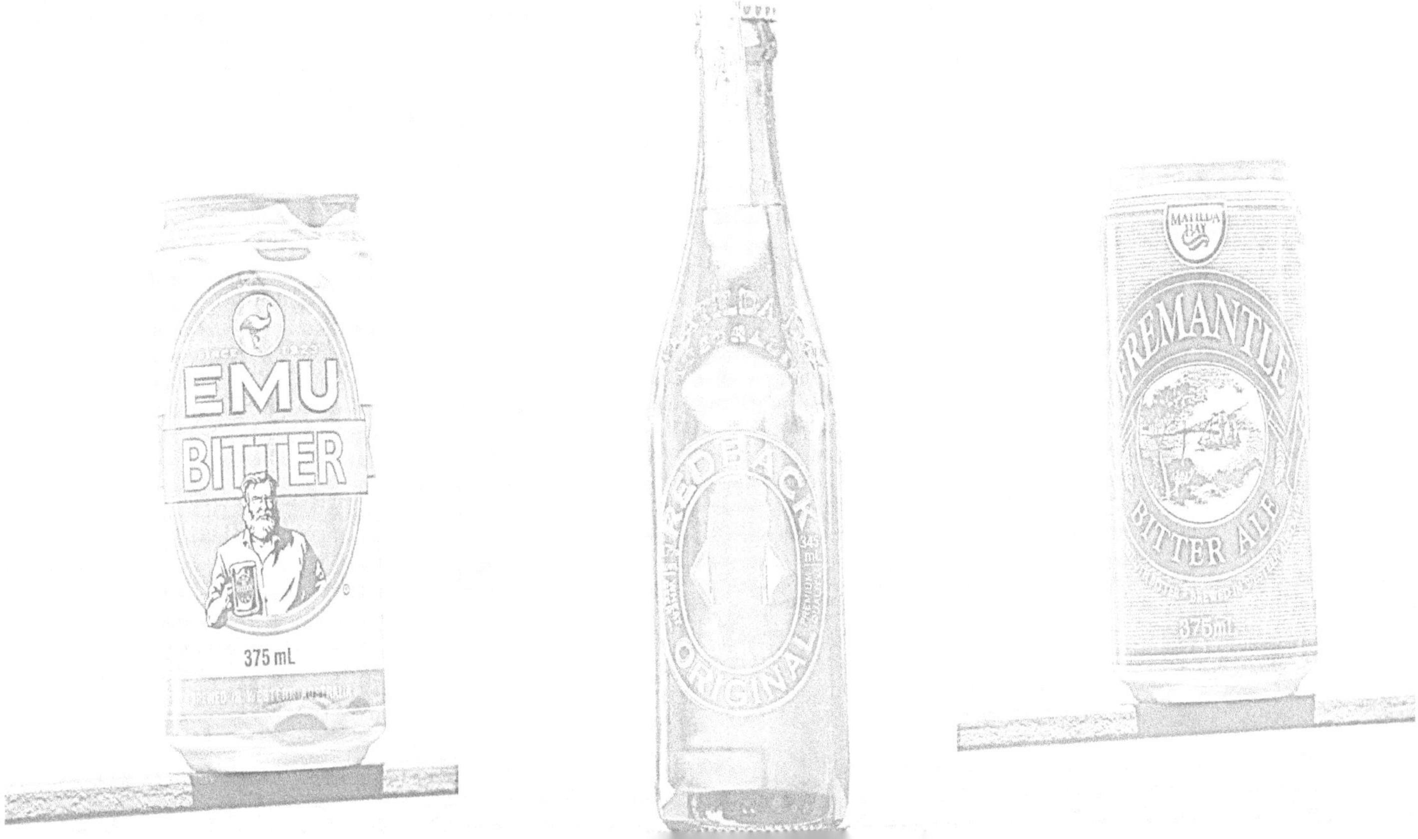
EMU
BITTER
375 mL
REDBACK
ORIGINAL
MATILDA BAY
FREMANTLE
BITTER ALE
375mL

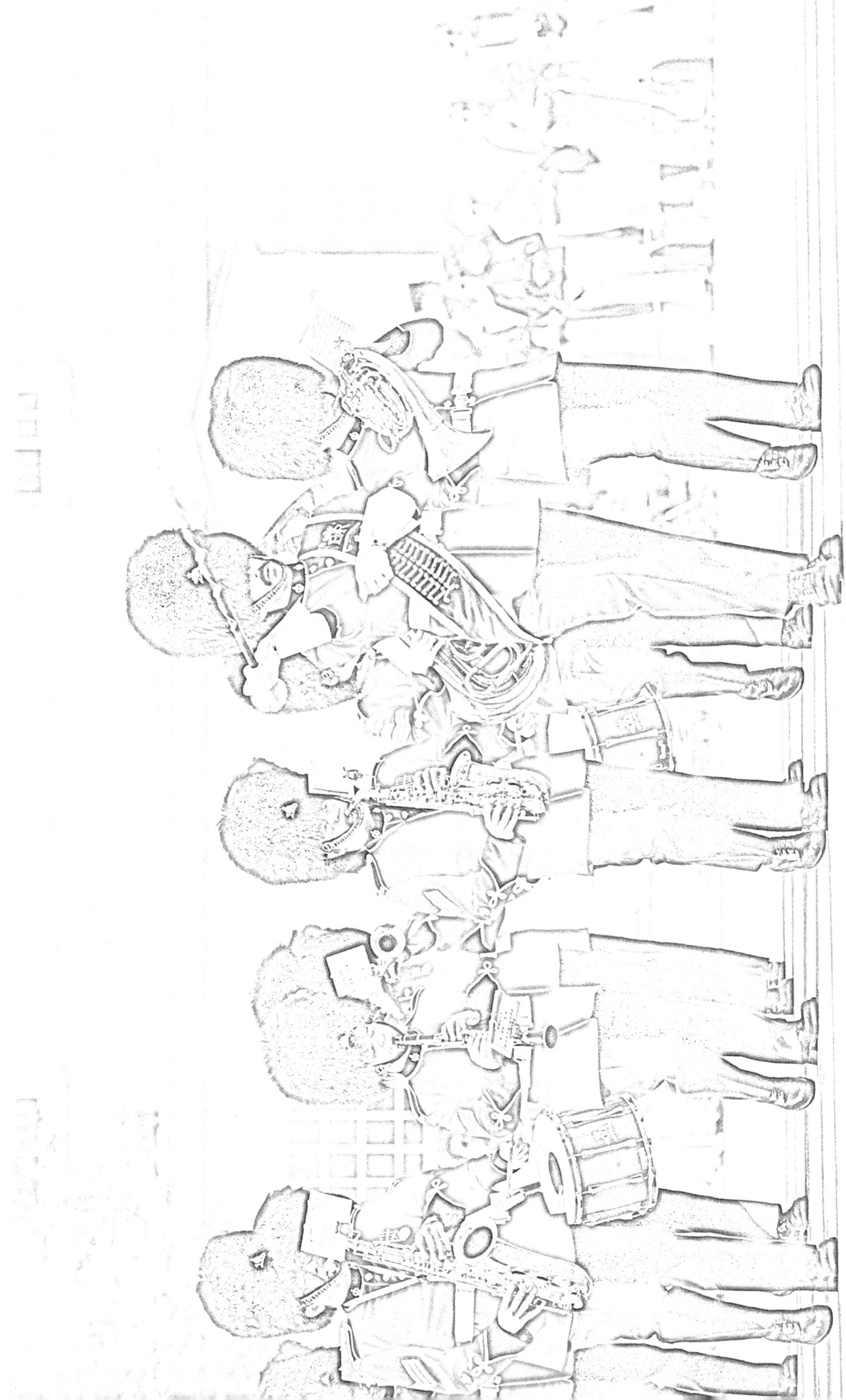

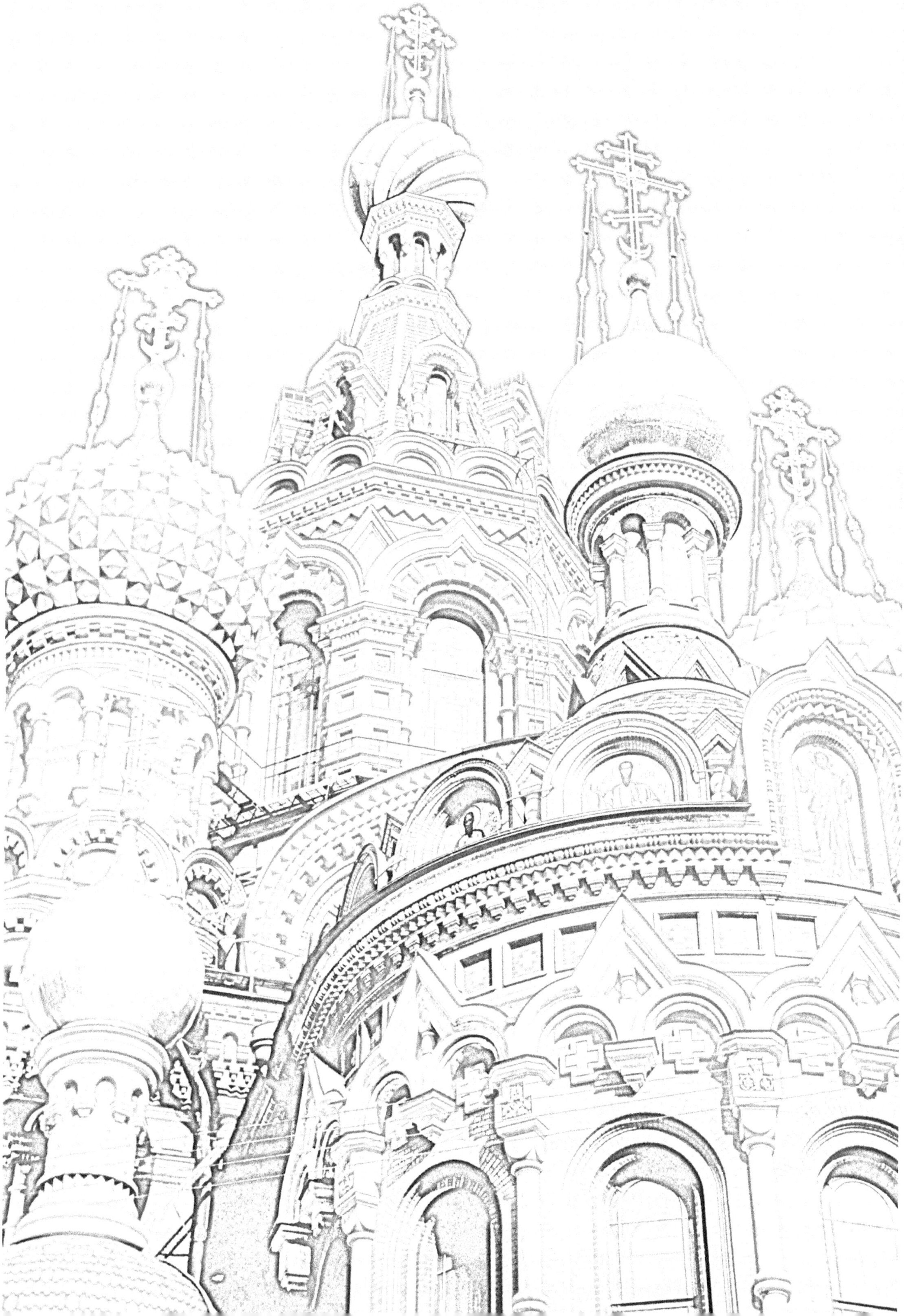

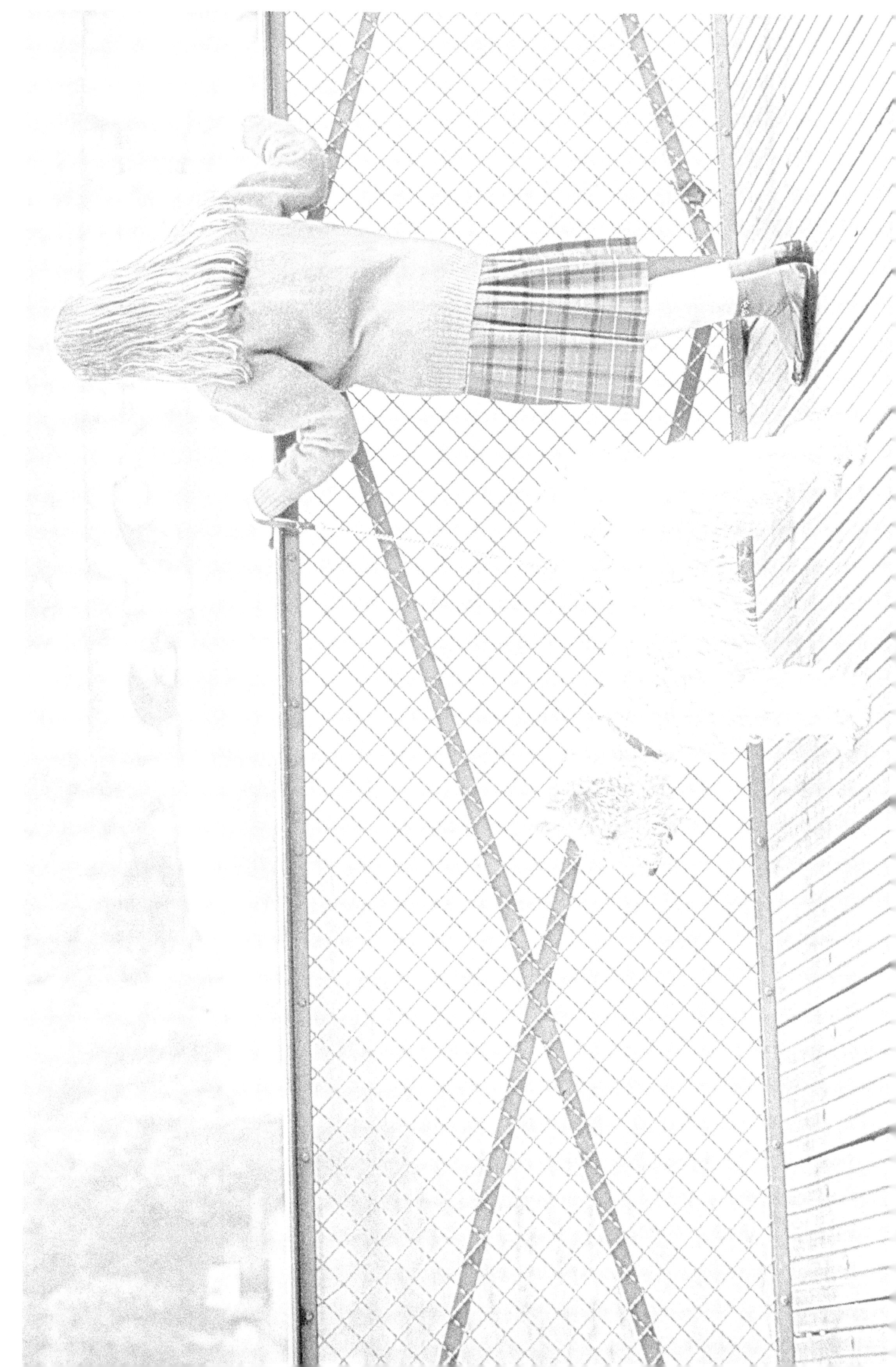

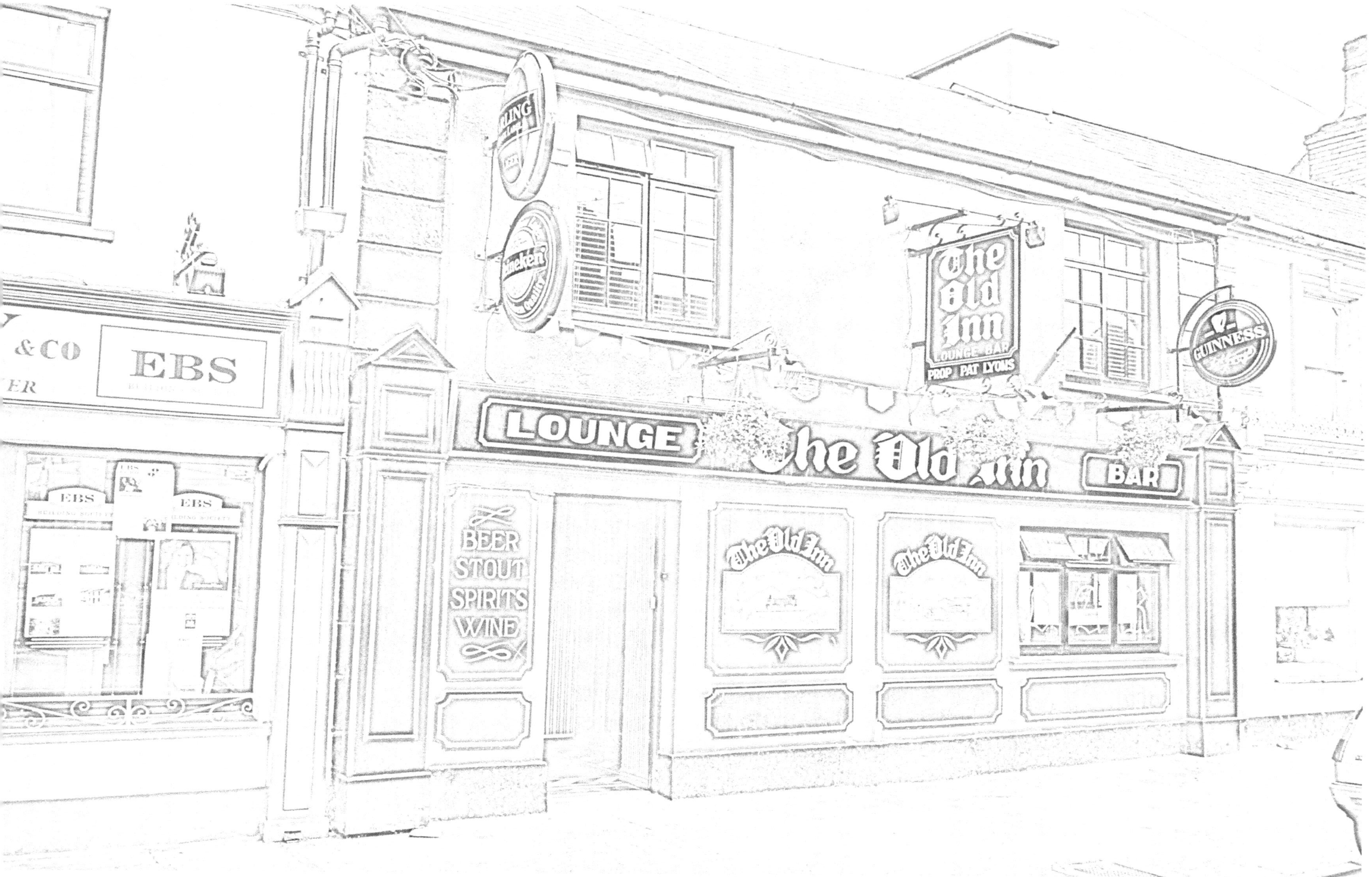

&CO
EBS
LOUNGE
The Old Inn
BAR
BEER
STOUT
SPIRITS
WINE
The Old Inn
The Old Inn
The Old Inn
LOUNGE BAR
PROP PAT LYONS
Heineken
GUINNESS

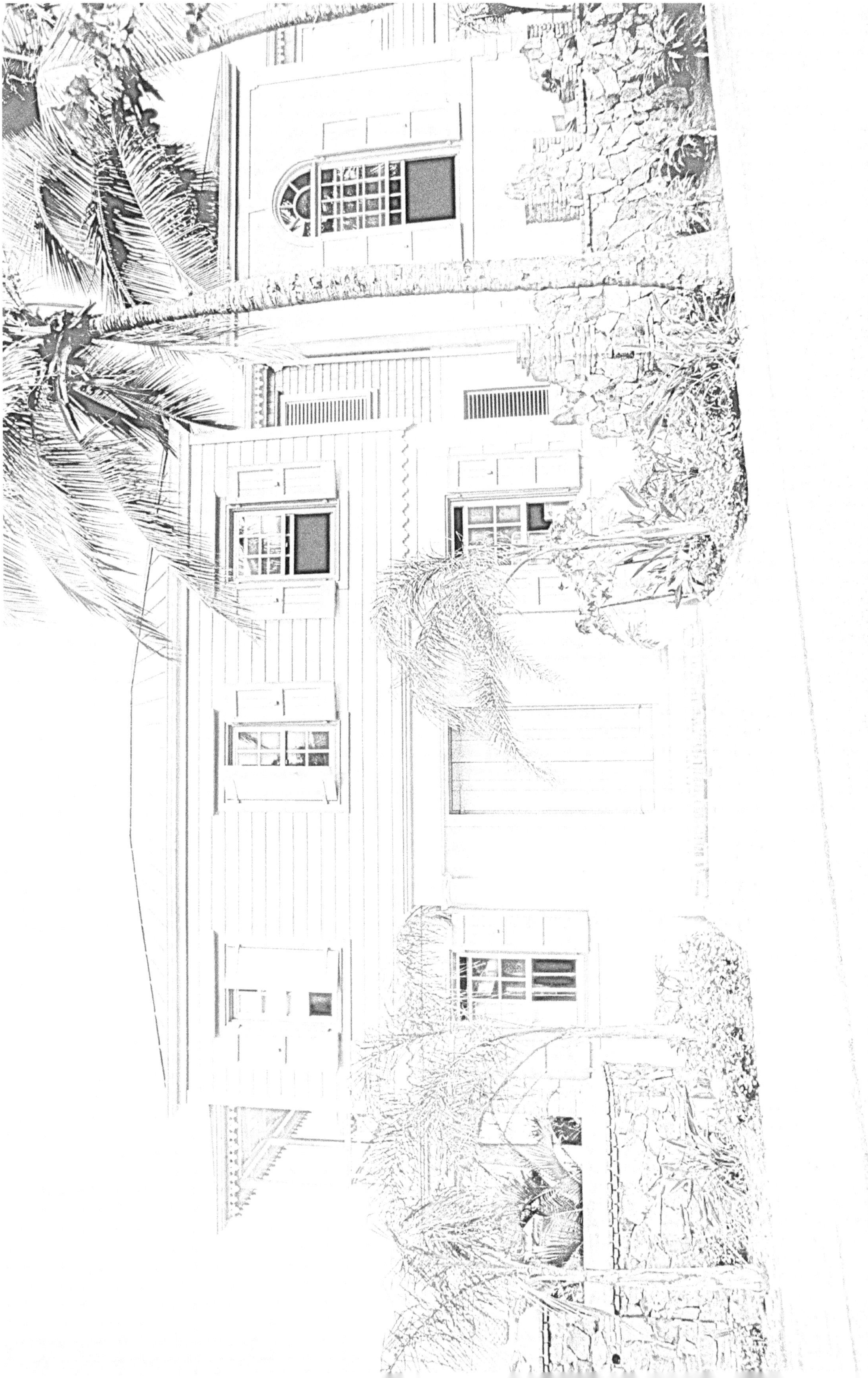

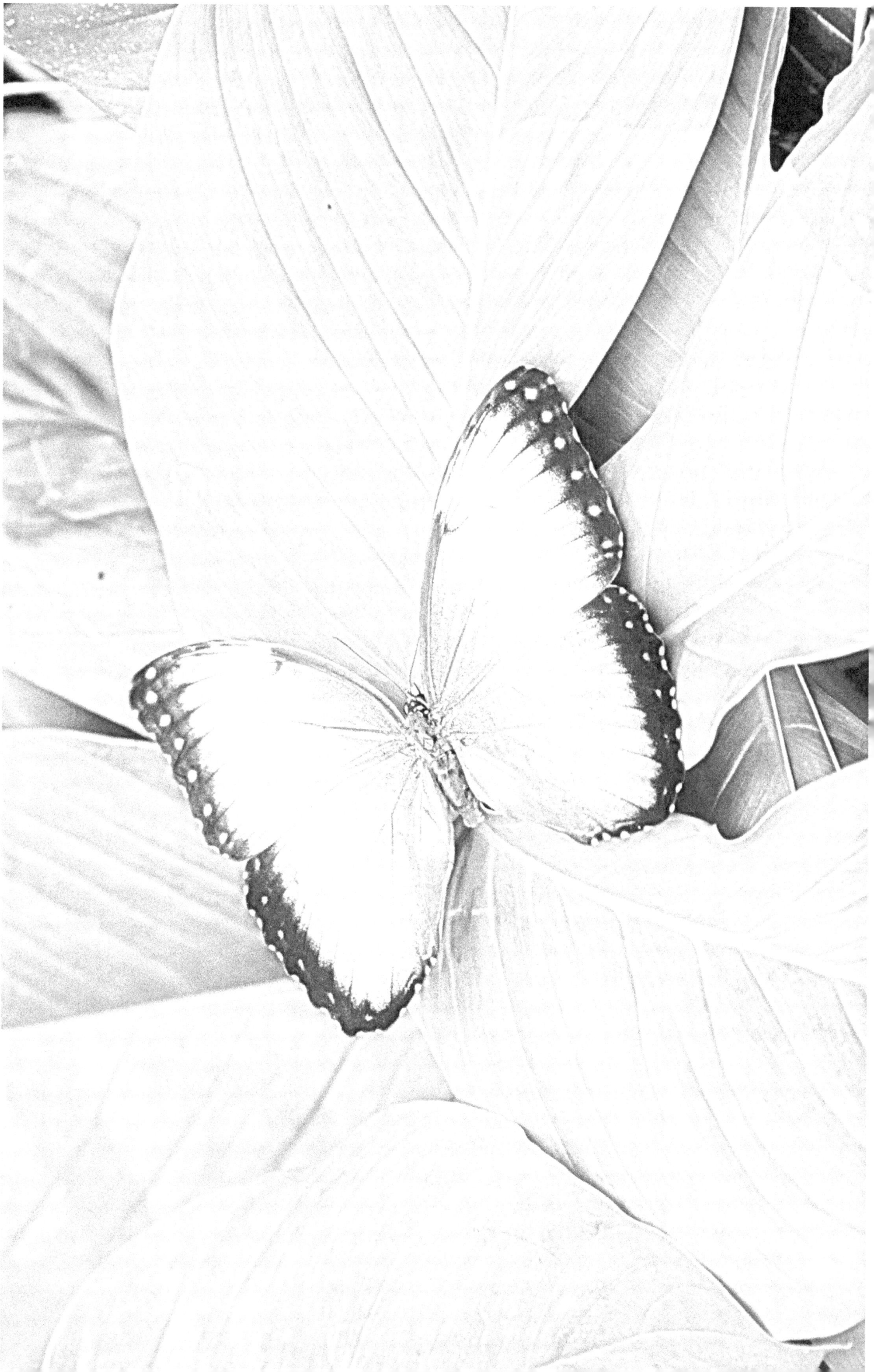

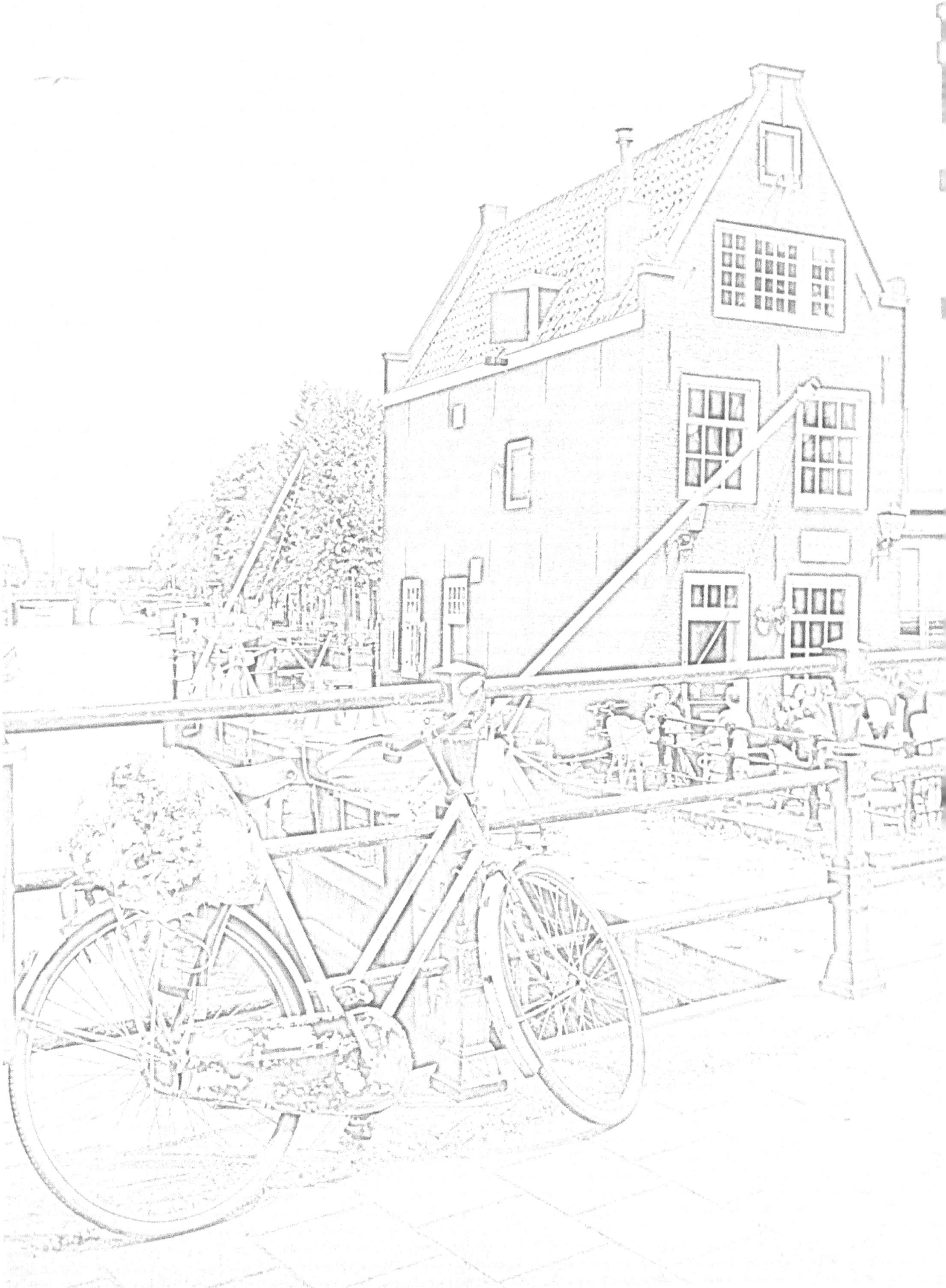

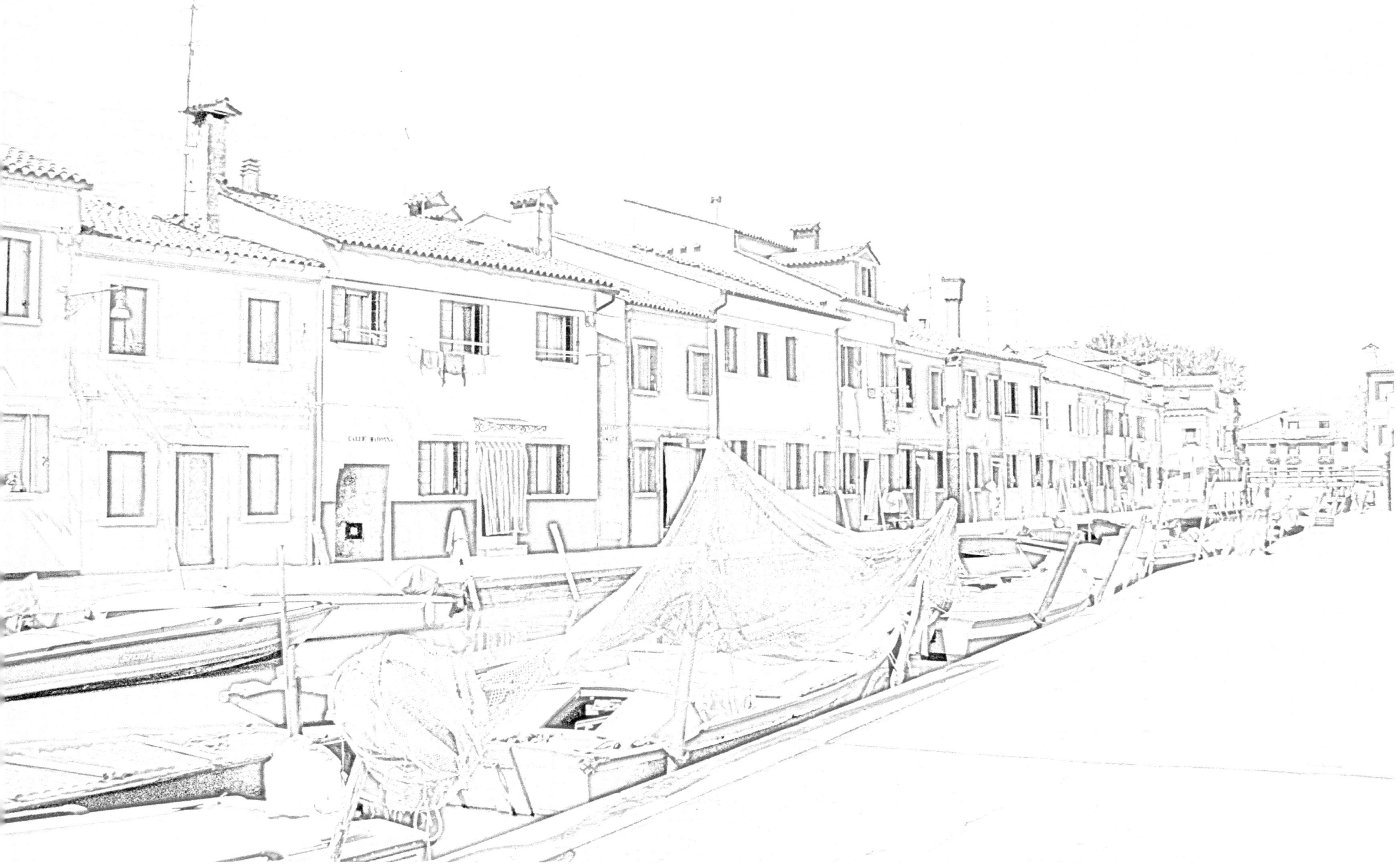

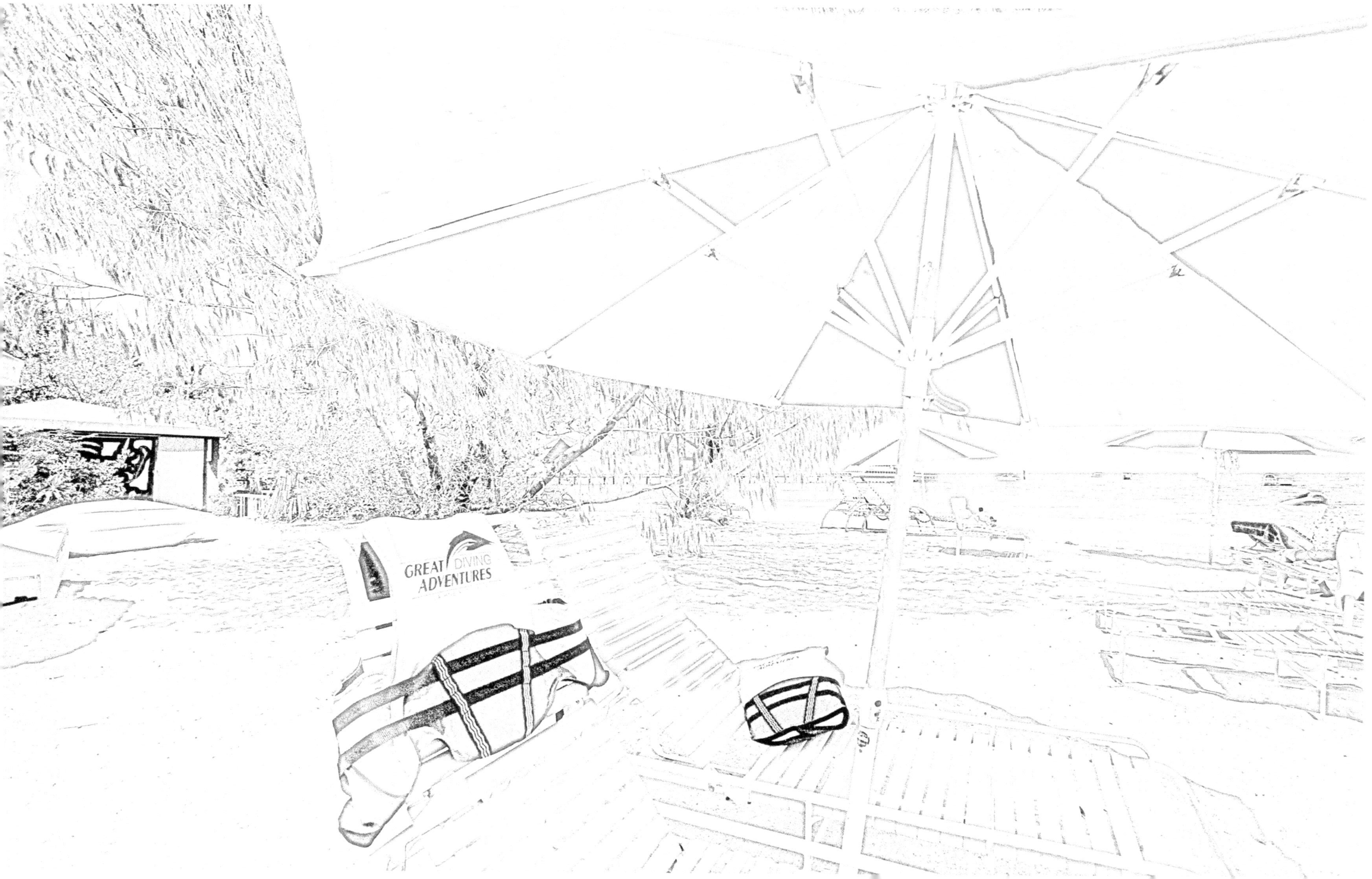
GREAT DIVING ADVENTURES

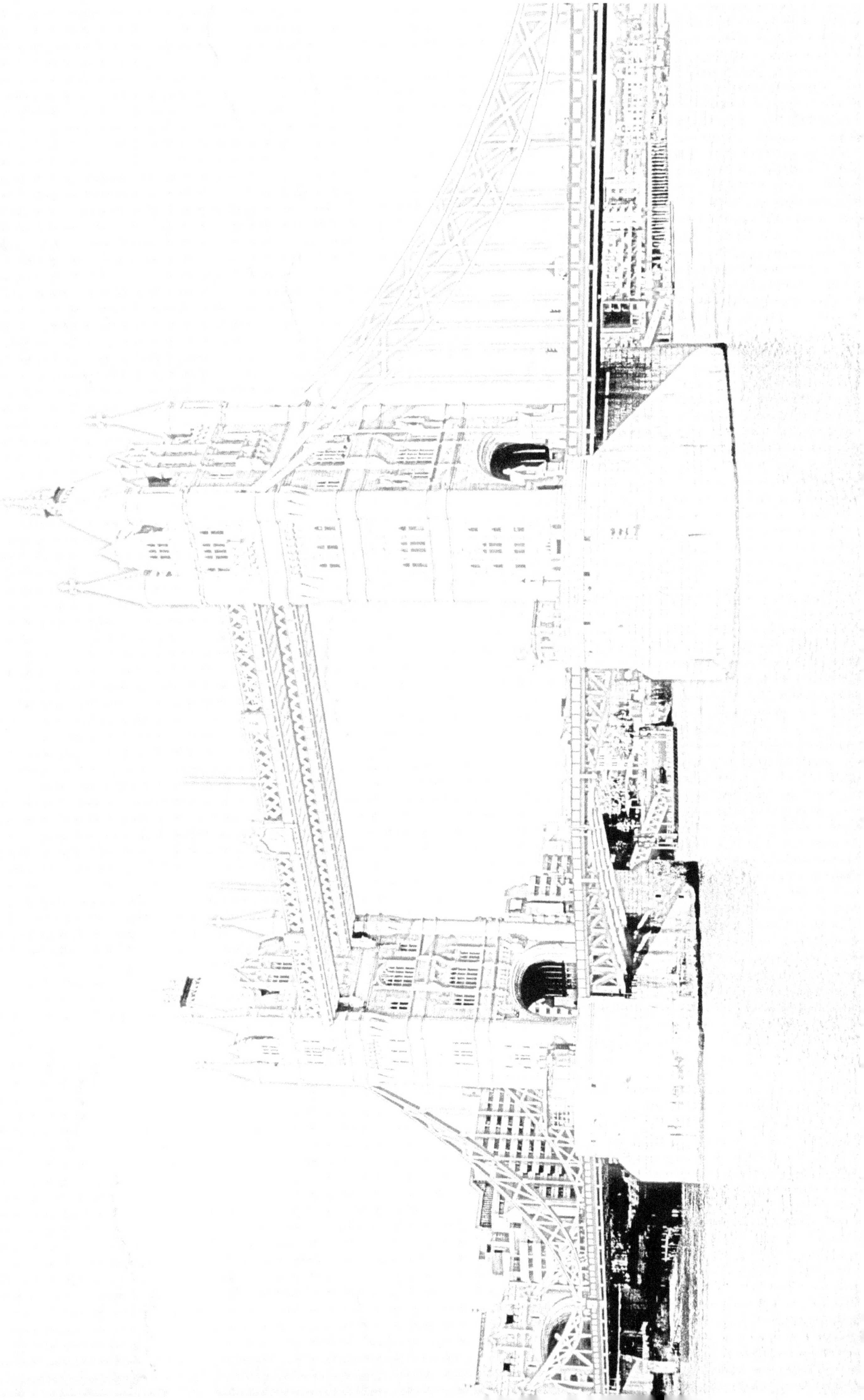

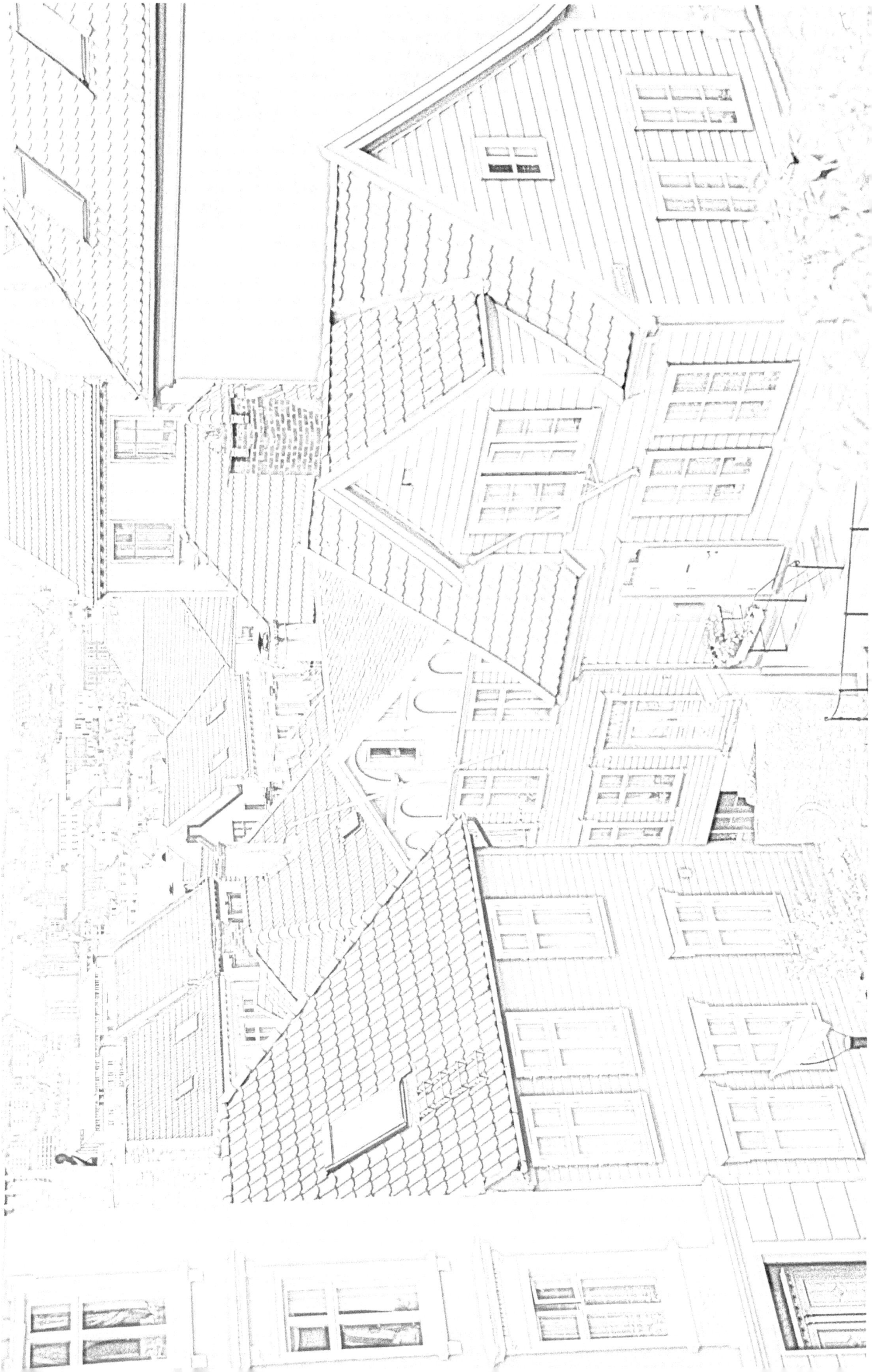

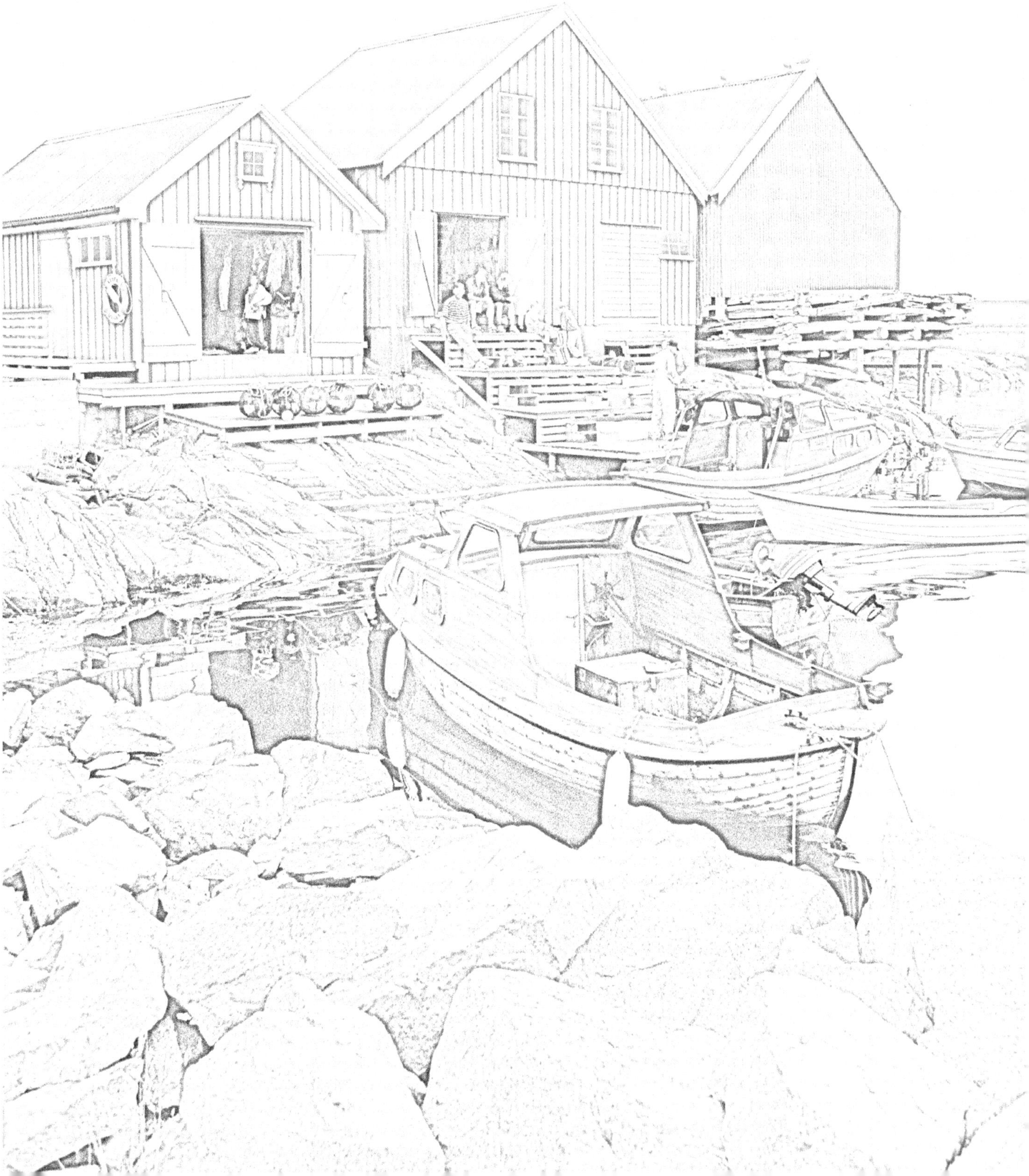

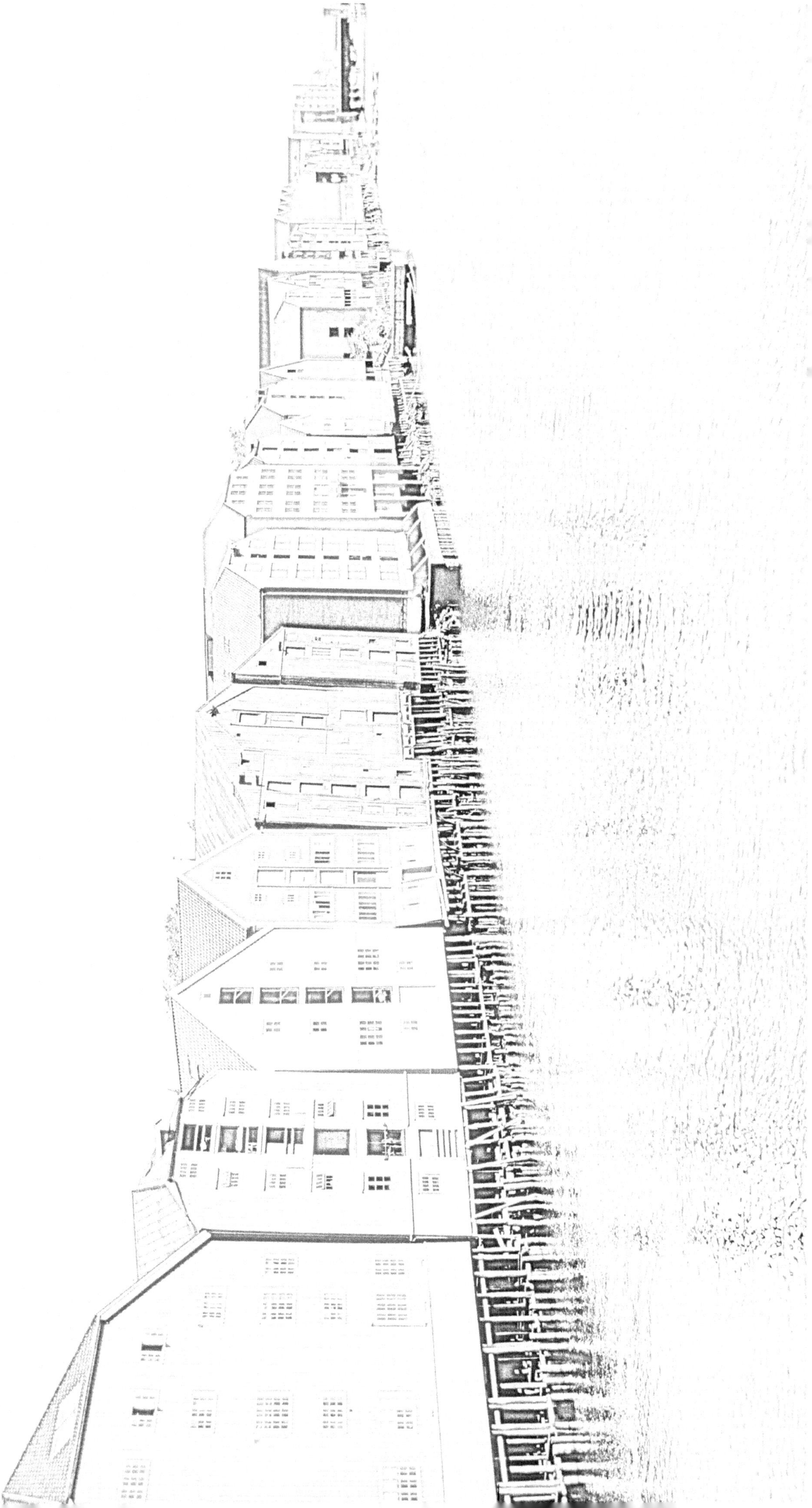

www.ingramcontent.com/pod-product-compliance
Lightning Source LLC
Chambersburg PA
CBHW081048180526
45170CB00005B/1737
* 9 7 8 0 3 5 9 7 9 3 7 9 2 *